Proprietary Rights and Insolvency in Sales Transactions

AUSTRALIA AND NEW ZEALAND
The Law Book Company Ltd.
Sydney : Melbourne : Perth

CANADA AND U.S.A.
The Carswell Company Ltd.
Agincourt, Ontario

INDIA
N. M. Tripathi Private Ltd.
Bombay
and
Eastern Law House Private Ltd.
Calcutta and Delhi
M.P.P. House
Bangalore

ISRAEL
Steimatzky's Agency Ltd.
Jerusalem : Tel Aviv : Haifa

PAKISTAN
Pakistan Law House
Karachi

Proprietary Rights and Insolvency in Sales Transactions

Second Edition

by

R. M. Goode, O.B.E., LL.D., F.B.A.

of Inner Temple, Barrister
(formerly a Solicitor of the Supreme Court (Hons.)),
Crowther Professor of Credit and Commercial Law
and Director of the Centre for Commercial Law Studies
Queen Mary College, University of London

London
Sweet & Maxwell
Centre for Commercial Law Studies
1989

Published in 1989 by
Sweet & Maxwell Limited of
South Quay Plaza, 183 Marsh Wall, London E14 9FT
Computerset by Promenade Graphics Ltd., Cheltenham
and Printed in Great Britain by
Butler and Tanner Limited
Frome, Somerset

British Library Cataloguing in Publication Data

Goode, R.M. (Royston Miles)
Proprietary rights and insolvency in sales
transactions.—2nd ed.
1. England. Goods. Sale. Contracts. Law
I. Title II. Queen Mary College. Centre for
Commercial Law Studies
344.206'72

ISBN 0-421-41010-8

Preface

The first edition of this book represented an attempt to provide a conceptual treatment of ownership and possession in relation to contracts of sale and to analyse the forms of real right capable of being created and the means by which such rights may be acquired and lost. The welcome given to the book indicated that such an analysis was found helpful both to practising lawyers and academic scholars.

In this new edition the structure of the book remains essentially the same but the text has been revised, expanded and updated and includes the most recent developments in this field.

I have taken the opportunity to correct a sprinkling of errors in the first edition, to develop the distinction between real and personal rights and to enlarge the treatment of the legal effect of commingling of goods, on which there have been two important recent decisions, namely *Indian Oil Corp. Ltd.* v. *Greenstone Shipping S.A. The Ypatiana* [1987] 2 Lloyd's Rep. 286, a decision of the English High Court, and *Coleman* v. *Harvey*, decided by the New Zealand Court of Appeal in March 1989.

The treatment of *Romalpa* clauses has given rise to continued discussions, debate and controversy, reflected in a revision of the text, which also deals with the impact of an administration petition and order under the Insolvency Act 1986 on the enforcement of rights under retention of title agreements. Although there are now a great many reported cases involving proprietary rights under contracts of sale, even the volume of these does not give a true picture of the significance of the subject, which forms part of the staple diet of liquidators, administrative receivers and administrators faced with claims of creditors asserting rights *in rem* over goods supplied under a contract of sale.

I should like to thank Professor David MacLauchlan of the Victoria University of Wellington for a helpful discussion on a number of points and for drawing my attention to a number of New Zealand cases; to Professor Terence Daintith, Director of the Institute of Advanced Legal Studies, for advising me on developments in oil and gas law; to the various reviewers of the first edition, not only for their kind reception of the book but also for their penetrating comments and criticisms; and, once again, to the publishers Sweet and Maxwell for all their labours in the production of the book.

The law is stated on the basis of materials available to me at May 1, 1989.

R. M. Goode

Centre for Commercial Law Studies
Queen Mary College
May 4, 1989

Preface to the First Edition

This book reproduces, with revisions and additions, the fourth series of Commercial Law Lectures, which I delivered at Queen Mary College in January and February 1985.

The contract of sale of goods is at once the most common and the most complex of all contracts, generating a mass of case law and an untold number of unreported disputes. I have taken as my theme the acquisition and loss of proprietary rights under contracts of sale, a subject which is of crucial importance in the light of the present number and magnitude of business insolvencies and which raises some of the most acute conceptual problems the practising lawyer is likely to encounter.

I have ventured into a number of areas on which there has hitherto been a dearth of legal analysis. Among these are: the concept of indirect constructive possession, where the bailor at will holds his rights on behalf of another; the acquisition of proprietary rights under contracts relating to oil, gas and minerals; the legal implications of the indemnity system currently employed to overcome delays in the delivery of bills of lading, and the potential impact of new technology relating to electronic processing of trade data; and the purchase of goods through an agent. I have also endeavoured to give what is, I hope, an accurate presentation of the current law governing reservation of title, rightly characterised by Staughton, J., as "a maze if not a minefield" (*Hendy Lennox (Industrial Engines) Ltd.* v. *Grahame Puttick Ltd.* [1984] 2 All E.R. 152 at p. 159). The Appendix contains the hitherto unpublished transcript of the important decision of Oliver J. (as he then was) in *The London Wine Company (Shippers) Ltd.* (1975).

I am indebted to a number of people for information and specimen documents. I should like to express my particular thanks to Francis Reynolds, of Worcester College, Oxford, for drawing my attention to the *Maynegrain* decision; to Julian Armstrong, of Esso Petroleum, Adrian Montague of Messrs. Linklaters and Paines, Mike Smith of Lloyd's Bank International, Krystyna Novak of Citibank N.A., Professor Michael Crommelin of Melbourne University, Professor Richard Bentham of the Centre for Petroleum Law Studies, Dundee University and Brian Youngman, former Deputy Legal Adviser to the National Coal Board, for their very helpful information on problems of oil, gas and minerals exploitation; John Wood of Mundogas, Alan Urbach of SeaDocs and Richard Dale of SITPRO, for enlightenment on the complexities of the indemnity system referred to above; Derek Kirby-Johnson, of Messrs. Monier Williams, for valuable information on the operation of string contracts; and Gerry Weiss of Cork Gully and Paul Shipperlee of Stoy Hayward for an insight into the practical problems created by reservation of title clauses. Once again, I should like to express my appreciation to the staff of Sweet & Maxwell for all their work on the production of this book.

The law is stated in the light of the materials available to me as at September 1, 1985.

Centre for Commercial Law Studies,
Queen Mary College.

R. M. Goode
September 1, 1985

Contents

TABLE OF CASES

TABLE OF STATUTES

I

Concepts of Ownership, Possession and Sale

The seller of goods collects the price and becomes insolvent before delivering them. Where does the buyer stand in relation to the seller's trustee or liquidator and the general body of creditors? The buyer of goods takes delivery and becomes insolvent without having paid the price. Can the seller recover the goods? The seller of goods which are in the possession of a carrier or warehouse gives instructions that part of the goods is to be set aside for a third party to whom the seller has contracted to sell them, and either the seller or the carrier or warehouse company becomes insolvent. What is the buyer's position?

These questions cannot be answered simply by the mechanical application of a set of rules laid down by statute. For one thing, many of the rules are not to be found in legislation; for another, it is only by a clear perception of the fundamental principles of ownership, possession and sale that the practising lawyer can offer reliable guidance where the circumstances presented for his consideration do not fall neatly within the confines of a decided case. I shall therefore devote this first lecture to an analysis of some fundamental concepts. These may seem abstract, but their practical relevance will soon become apparent.

1. THE NATURE AND SIGNIFICANCE OF REAL RIGHTS

Real and personal rights

A person has a real right in goods where he has an absolute or limited interest in them or a right to have the goods or their proceeds applied towards satisfaction of an obligation owed to him. Real rights may thus take one of three forms:

(1) Ownership, whether by holding the best title or by holding possession *animo domini*[1] and whether holding absolutely or as mortgagee.

(2) Possession for a limited interest, *i.e.* as bailee under some form of bailment,[2] whether directly or through another (shared, or constructive, possession[3]).

[1] See p. 4.
[2] See p. 7.
[3] See p. 8.

(3) Real security not based on ownership or possession, *i.e.* a charge[4] or non-possessory lien.[5]

But a mere agreement to deliver possession does not confer real rights. Thus if A, who is the owner of goods and in possession of them, agrees to deliver them to B, then until B acquires either ownership or possession he has no real rights in the goods, merely a personal right to call for their transfer to him. Even a court order requiring A to deliver the goods to B does not confer on B a real right in the goods. This can come about only as the result of A complying with the order or B enforcing it.

A person cannot have a real right in goods unless they have been identified. Where the goods are wholly unascertained, in the sense that not even the source of supply is identified by contract or by rules of law, he has merely a personal right to call for the delivery to him of such weight, quantity or number as suffices to discharge the undertaking of the party who agreed to deliver them. Where his entitlement is to an unidentified part of a bulk, or source of supply,[6] then until the goods have become ascertained by some act of appropriation he has merely a personal right to delivery of the requisite weight, quantity or number from the bulk or source of supply. However, it is necessary to distinguish a right to an unidentified part of a bulk from a part interest in the entire bulk. A right to be given 12 bottles from a cellar containing 100 bottles is not at all the same thing as a 12 per cent. interest in the entire collection of 100 bottles. In the first case, the right is a purely personal right to delivery of 12 unidentified bottles. In the second, the party is co-owner of the bulk to the extent of a 12 per cent. share. The distinction is crucial and is one to which I shall return.[7]

The significance of real rights

If it were not for the possibility of the insolvency of A or B, the distinction between a real right *in* goods and a personal right *to* goods would be largely academic, since B could procure by seizure or court order either the attainment of the real right for which he had bargained or its monetary value by way of damages. What makes the

4 That is, a mere charge, as opposed to a charge embodied in an equitable mortgage. See R. M. Goode, *Legal Problems of Credit and Security* (2nd ed., 1988), p. 14. A charge may be created by agreement (though only in equity) or by statute.

5 There are three kinds of non-possessory lien: the equitable lien, the statutory lien and the maritime lien.

6 The source is usually identified by the terms of the contract or by some post-contract act of quasi-appropriation provided for by the contract, *e.g.* shipment of the goods as an unidentified part of a bulk cargo. It is also possible however, to have identification of the source by rules of law, as where under equitable rules of tracing a person is given an equitable charge over a fund of assets in which the goods to which he is entitled or their proceeds have become mingled.

7 See below, pp. 21 *et seq.*

distinction between real and personal rights of enormous significance is the principle of insolvency law that only the assets of the bankrupt or company in liquidation are available for distribution among creditors. Accordingly if one party becomes insolvent, the other may enforce a real right against the insolvent party's estate, so far as this does not conflict with a stronger real right in the insolvent party, and may accordingly withhold or recover the goods from the insolvent party's trustee[8] and the general body of creditors,[9] but any personal right against the insolvent party is converted into a right to prove for its monetary value in competition with other creditors, a right which may be worth little or nothing where the assets are insufficient to cover the liabilities and insolvency costs.

It is for this reason that it may be vital to a creditor to be able to establish that he owns or holds possession of goods that would otherwise form part of the insolvent party's estate. If he is the beneficial owner with the best right to possession, he can retain the goods, if they are in his possession, or recover them from the party who is in possession. If his interest is the limited interest of a bailee, he is likewise entitled to assert it and to hold possession against the owner's trustee upon the terms of the bailment. Where the terms of the bailment provide for ownership to pass to him in due course, whether automatically on payment (as under a conditional sale agreement) or on exercise of an option to purchase (as under a hire-purchase agreement), he can enforce those provisions against the trustee. To assert his rights as a possessor, the bailee need not be in physical possession; it suffices that he holds constructive possession in the sense described below.

By contrast, a claimant who has a mere personal right to call for the transfer of ownership or the delivery of possession must normally content himself with proof as an unsecured creditor in the insolvent's estate. To this rule there are a few exceptions discussed below.

Ownership

For our purposes ownership may be defined as title to the absolute interest in goods, "absolute interest" denoting the residue of rights remaining in a person, or in persons concurrently, after specific rights over the goods have been granted to others.[10] Ownership may be legal or equitable. In contrast to land, in which an indefinite number of legal estates and interests may subsist at any one time because a smaller legal title can be carved out of a larger, ownership

[8] Except where otherwise indicated, the word "trustee" is used throughout to denote the trustee in bankruptcy of an individual or the liquidator of a company.

[9] Subject to restrictions imposed by the Insolvency Act 1986 during the pendency of a petition for an administration order and the currency of any administration order made. See below, p. 108.

[10] See R. M. Goode, *Commercial Law*, (1985), pp. 52 *et seq.*

of goods is indivisible.[11] Legal title may be held by persons concurrently, as joint tenants or tenants in common, but it is not possible to split the title by transferring limited legal interests derived from it; title to goods may only be transferred as a whole. However, while a limited legal interest cannot be derived from the full legal title, possession with the intention of asserting rights of ownership constitutes an independent and original source of title. Due to the significance attached to possession by the common law, a person in possession with the intention of asserting ownership is treated in law as an owner, and is entitled to have his possession protected, against all persons except the true owner or those claiming under him or by his authority. Thus under English law it is possible for two, and only two, absolute legal interests to subsist in goods at the same time: the best title, held by the person who is the true owner in the sense that he has the best right to the goods, and the second best (or relative) title, obtained by taking or holding possession *animo domini*. It is important to bear in mind that both titles are original; the title obtained by possession is not carved out of, or derived from, the title of the true owner but is an independent legal title. I have thought it worth while dwelling on these points since the Sale of Goods Act 1979 implicitly recognises the relativity of title; indeed, many of its provisions can be understood only once it is appreciated that two concurrent legal titles are possible and that a sale by a "non-owner" (in the sense of one who lacks the best title) is nevertheless a sale for the purpose of the Act if made by a person in possession *animo domini*.

For the purpose of insolvency law, a bare legal title, such as that vested in a bare trustee under a passive trust,[12] is disregarded. If A, who is in possession of goods as bare trustee for B, becomes insolvent, B is entitled to recover them.[13] Conversely, if B were in possession holding a bare legal title, he would have to surrender the goods to A's trustee. The position would be otherwise if B was a trustee under an active trust, with powers of management, or held the legal title for an interest of his own, *e.g.* as mortgagee. In either case, he would be entitled to retain the goods so long as, in the former case, his management powers under the trust continued and, in the latter case, the mortgage remained unredeemed. In the ensuing analysis, I shall use the term "ownership" to denote the interest of a party who is the beneficial owner and either holds the legal title or has the immediate right to call for it to be vested in him. The first of

[11] Goode, *op. cit.*, pp. 54 *et seq.*

[12] A bare trustee under a passive trust is one who has no powers of management over the trust property and whose sole function is to hold such property to the order of the beneficiary, who may at any time terminate the trust and require the trustee to make over the property to him.

[13] But see n. 9, above.

these cases will be referred to as "legal ownership," the second as "equitable ownership."

(1) *Legal ownership*

For legal ownership to pass from A to B by act of parties, A must make a present transfer of existing goods which he currently owns or of which he has a power to dispose. If the goods belong to O but A is authorised to dispose of them, and does so within the limits of his authority, then A's disposition is an exercise of both a power and a right of disposal, and ownership unquestionably passes to B as if the disposition had been made by O personally. But there may be cases where, by some exception to the *nemo dat* rule, A can effectively transfer to B a good title to O's goods even though in making the transfer A exceeded his authority or, indeed, acted without having any authority at all. In such cases, A's disposition is a breach of his duty to O and makes him liable to O in damages but O's title is effectively overridden in favour of B. This can happen at common law where A is held out by O as having authority to sell and acts within the limits of his ostensible authority. There are also various statutory exceptions to the *nemo dat* rule, *e.g.* a sale in market overt, a sale by a seller who is allowed to remain in possession and makes a wrongful second disposition, a sale by a buyer in possession before he himself has acquired title, and so on. These exceptions to the *nemo dat* rule are examined in detail in the standard textbooks[14] and I need not refer to them further at this point, though some of them will be relevant to issues discussed later.

In general, a person cannot transfer legal ownership to future goods, that is, goods which he neither owns nor possesses at the time of the transfer. Even when he subsequently acquires the goods, ownership will not pass at law without a new dispositive act, and until this has been done the transferee's ownership will be purely equitable. To this general rule there is an exception particularly relevant to the theme of these lectures, namely the contract of sale of goods. The effect of the Sale of Goods Act 1979, re-enacting the Sale of Goods Act 1893, is that legal title to future goods will vest automatically on their acquisition by the seller, if the parties so intend, without the need for any new act of transfer.[15]

(2) *Equitable ownership*

Equitable ownership may arise from a trust, as where O declares himself a trustee of goods for B or transfers the goods to A to hold on

[14] See, for example, R. M. Goode, *Commercial Law*, Chap. 15; *Benjamin's Sale of Goods* (3rd ed.), Chap. 7.

[15] Sale of Goods Act 1979, s.2(5), (6).

trust for B. Equitable ownership may also be conferred on B as the result of an uncompleted agreement to transfer ownership to him or as the result of a purported transfer which is ineffective because the intending transferor has neither ownership nor a power of disposal. Again, the contract of sale is an important exception. The effect of the Sale of Goods Act appears to be that until the property (*i.e.* legal ownership) has passed to the buyer pursuant to the contract, he has merely a personal contractual right to call for the transfer to be made to him, and nothing more.[16] So whereas an agreement for a mortgage usually constitutes an equitable mortgage and an agreement for the sale of land makes the vendor a trustee for the purchaser, an agreement for sale of goods does not of itself vest equitable ownership in the buyer or, indeed, confer any real right on him at all. It is, of course, open to the parties to agree upon a trust, equitable charge or equitable assignment in favour of the buyer, but the mere conclusion of an agreement to sell does not by itself produce this effect.

Co-ownership

Goods, like land, may be the subject of co-ownership at law and in equity. Two or more persons may hold legal co-ownership either as joint tenants[17] or as tenants in common.[18] Ownership in common typically arises where products belonging to different owners become commingled, as in the case of gas or oil brought ashore in a pipeline,[19] or where a conditional buyer of goods commingles them with his own goods or those of a third party.[20] Severance of a joint tenancy results in a legal[21] tenancy in common. Equitable co-ownership may also take the form either of a joint tenancy or a tenancy in common, the strong presumption being in favour of the latter. An equitable joint tenancy presupposes that the legal title is in a third party who holds for the co-owners as joint tenants. An equitable

[16] Though there is no authority directly on this point, there are powerful dicta to that effect. See *Re Wait* [1927] 1 Ch. 606, *per* Atkin L.J., at pp. 635–636; *Leigh and Sillivan Ltd.* v. *Aliakmon Shipping Co. Ltd. (The Aliakmon)* [1986] A.C. 785, *per* Lord Brandon at p. 812; *Re London Wine Co. (Shippers) Ltd.* (1975), unreported, Oliver J., reproduced in the Appendix at pp. 111 *et seq.* and discussed *post*, pp. 22 *et seq.*

[17] *Re Wait*, above, *per* Atkin L.J. at p. 636.

[18] See Crossley Vaines, *Personal Property* (5th ed.), Chap. 5. A particular feature of an unsevered legal joint tenancy is that on the death of one joint the asset passes to the other or others by survivorship.

[19] See below, p. 35.

[20] See below, pp. 71, 85, 90.

[21] In this respect, co-ownership of goods differs from that of land, of which it is no longer possible to have a legal tenancy in common (Law of Property Act 1925, ss.1(6), 34(1), 36(2)).

tenancy in common may arise in the same way or as the result of the co-owners taking the legal title as joint tenants but holding it for themselves in equity as tenants in common.[22]

Possession

As previously stated, possession is itself a real right, exercisable against everyone except a person having a better right to possession. A person who, though not the owner, holds possession with the intention of asserting ownership is treated by the law as the owner, and as entitled to legal protection as such, against everyone except the true owner or a person deriving title through or under him or acting with his authority. Since the true owner usually shows up, we can for practical purposes disregard this second best possessory title.[23] This leaves us with the possessory rights of the holder of a limited interest, *i.e.* a bailee who is in possession not as mere custodian but for an interest of his own, *e.g.* under a pledge, a lien or a hiring, hire-purchase or conditional sale agreement.

It is important to note that what confers a real right on the bailee in the first instance is not the agreement pursuant to which possession is to be given to him but the delivery of possession itself. For example, an agreement to supply equipment on lease for five years does not of itself give the intended lessee a right *in rem*, and if the lessor were to become bankrupt before delivering possession the lessee's remedy would be restricted to a proof in the bankruptcy. Once possession has been given to the lessee, thereby conferring on him a real right in the leased goods, the quantum of that right is measured by the terms of the leasing agreement, so that he may hold possession against the trustee for the rest of the five-year period.

It follows that where one of the parties to a contract for the sale of goods becomes insolvent, the question who has possession and on what terms is just as important as who has ownership. If the contract under which possession is taken is an agreement for sale, the buyer, as potential owner, has the right to perpetual possession, subject to compliance with the terms of the contract, and may complete the transaction by tendering the price. Similarly, where the seller has transferred title to the buyer, who becomes insolvent without having paid the price, the seller may yet be able to protect himself by exercising a lien if he is still in possession or a right to stop the goods in transit if they have not yet reached the buyer's possession.[24]

[22] There is a presumption to this effect where the co-owners have contributed the price in unequal shares (*Wray* v. *Steele* (1814) 2 Ves. & B. 388; *Re A Policy No. 6402 of Scottish Equitable Life Assurance Society* [1902] 1 Ch. 282.

[23] See Goode *op. cit.* n. 14 above, pp. 52 *et seq.*

[24] Sale of Goods Act 1979, ss.39–46.

Relevance of possession to transfer of ownership

Though possession is a concept distinct from ownership, and the passing of property under a contract of sale does not depend upon delivery,[25] the holding or delivery of possession may be relevant to the acquisition or transfer of ownership. We have already seen[26] that the possessor holding *animo domini* is treated by the law as an owner. In addition, several exceptions to the *nemo dat* rule turn on possession. For example, where a seller wrongfully sells the same goods to two successive buyers the second buyer may obtain priority under section 24 of the Sale of Goods Act, but only if the seller remained in possession after the first sale and delivered possession to the second buyer under the second contract of sale. Again, a buyer who resells goods before he has himself become the owner may thereby pass a good title to the sub-purchaser under section 25 of the Act, but only if the first buyer obtained possession and delivered possession to the second buyer. But physical possession is not essential; constructive possession suffices.[27]

Forms of possession

There are three principal forms of possession of goods in law. The first is physical possession. The second is possession of goods giving physical control, *e.g.* the keys to the warehouse in which the goods are stored. The third is possession through a bailee at will, that is, a carrier, warehouseman or other physical possessor who agrees to hold the goods to the bailor's order. This is the so-called constructive, or shared, possession. The bailee at will has physical control but not for any interest of his own; he holds the goods entirely at his bailor's pleasure, his possession is that of his bailor and legal control thus lies with the bailor. Like ownership, possession of chattels is indivisible. Possession may be shared but there is only one jointly held possessory interest, not two separate interests.[28]

The bailor's constructive possession depends for its creation and subsistence on the will of the bailee. If he decides to assert an interest of his own, whether by acting as owner or by asserting a lien or other limited interest, then for so long as he does so he holds exclusive possession and the bailor regains constructive possession only if and when the bailee once again consents to accept the status of bailee at will. The archetypal bailment at will is the gratuitous bailment, which exists exclusively for the benefit of the bailor. But

[25] See Sale of Goods Act 1979, s.18, rule 1.

[26] Above, p. 4.

[27] See, for example, *Four Point Garage Ltd.* v. *Carter* [1985] 3 All E.R. 12; *Gamer's Motor Centre (Newcastle) Pty. Ltd.* v. *Natwest Wholesale Australia Pty. Ltd.* (1987) 61 A.L.J.R. 415. As to constructive possession, see below.

[28] For a fuller discussion, see R. M. Goode, *Commercial Law*, (1985), pp. 61–62.

even a bailee under a bailment for reward—such as a carrier or warehouseman—can be a bailee at will, holding possession solely for the interest of his bailor, as where the bailee collects payment for his services in advance or relies on the creditworthiness of his bailor or a third party and is willing to release the goods before being paid. Where the bailee does assert a lien, exclusive possession remains in him until the lien is discharged and he is willing to release the goods to the bailor's order, whereupon the bailor acquires constructive possession.

Attornment

Where A, having initially held goods for himself, agrees to continue in possession as B's bailee, he is said to "attorn" to B, that is, to recognise B as the person having legal control of the goods.[29] So A, after selling goods to B, may hold them for B to collect at his pleasure. In this way, A's exclusive possession becomes converted into a shared possession, A holding physical possession in right of B, who has constructive possession. Similarly, if T, having received the goods as A's bailee, agrees with B that he will thereafter hold them to B's order, T thereby attorns to B, who displaces A as joint possessor. The typical case is where A sells goods to B, instructing T to release them to B, and T notifies B that the goods are available for collection.

A particular form of attornment is the issue of a document of title giving legal control of the goods. I shall say more about documents of title later. Suffice it to mention that to give control it must be issued or accepted by the bailee of goods, must thereby embody his undertaking to hold the goods for, and release them to, whoever presents the document and must be recognised by statute or mercantile usage as a document which enables control of the goods to pass by delivery of the document with any necessary indorsement. Such a document of title (and, as will be seen, not all documents of title do give control in this way) is in effect an attornment in

[29] See Goode *op. cit.* pp. 62–63, 221, 759–760. Where A's attornment is by way of pledge effected by delivery of a document—*e.g.* a warehouse receipt—the document constitutes a bill of sale which is registrable under the Bills of Sale Acts 1878–1891 (or where A is a company, under s.395 of the Companies Act 1985) unless falling within one of the exemptions, *e.g.* as a document used in the ordinary course of business as proof of the possession or control of goods (Bills of Sale Act 1878, s.4). See *Dublin City Distillery (Great Brunswick Street, Dublin) Ltd.* v. *Doherty* [1914] A.C. 823. The position is otherwise where the pledge takes effect by physical delivery of the goods on the terms of an accompanying document embodying the terms of the pledge. In such a case, it is not the document that effects the transfer, and the Bills of Sale Acts do not apply (*Wrightson* v. *McArthur & Hutchisons (1919) Ltd.* [1921] 2 K.B. 807).

advance. The undertaking to each transferee of the document is embodied in the document itself and does not have to be given separately after the transfer has taken place.

From the fact that the bill of lading is the only document of title known to the common law it would seem to follow that no other form of advance attornment is recognized. In *Farina* v. *Home*[30] it was held that the issue of a transferable delivery warrant by a wharfinger in favour of the consignee of the goods did not constitute constructive delivery to an indorsee of the warrant until the wharfinger had attorned to him. If this be the case as regards transferable warrants, then *a fortiori* an undertaking by T which is merely oral, or is embodied in a non-transferable document, to hold goods to A or his order does not constitute an attornment in advance in favour of B consequent on A's direction to T to hold the goods for B.

The effect of an attornment is to commit the person in physical possession to make delivery to his new bailor. Frequently the attornment will create a contract between the bailee and his new bailor. Where goods are held by a warehouse or carrier, it is a common condition of any attornment that the new bailor will be responsible for warehouse charges or freight, and even where this is not expressly agreed the courts are very ready to imply such an undertaking.[31] This constitutes the consideration for the bailee's promise to deliver to the new bailor and thus commits the bailee to the bailor by contract. However, this is not an essential condition of liability. By informing the new bailor that the goods will be held to his order the bailee makes his own possession that of the new bailor and thus becomes estopped from disputing the latter's right to the goods. Since the effect of the attornment is thus to confer on the new bailor a real right in the goods, *i.e.* constructive possession, the normal requirement for an estoppel, that the representee has acted in reliance on the representation, would not appear to apply. Certainly the leading cases on attornment do not suggest that the new bailor has to do more than show the bailee's acknowledgment that he is now holding the goods for the new bailor.[32]

[30] (1846) 6 M. & W. 119.

[31] *Swan* v. *Barber* (1879) 5 Ex.D. 130; *Sanders* v. *Vanzeller* (1843) 4 Q.B. 260. *Brandt* v. *Liverpool, Brazil and River Plate Steam Navigation Co. Ltd.* [1924] 1 K.B. 575. See further below, p. 63.

[32] See, for example, *Dublin City Distillery (Great Brunswick Street, Dublin) Ltd.* v. *Doherty, supra*; *Laurie & Morewood* v. *John Dudin & Sons* [1925] 2 K.B. 383. In *Knights* v. *Wiffen* (1870) 5 L.R. Q.B. 660 it appears to have been assumed that the estoppel was created as the result of the plaintiff's change of position, but in that case the goods in question had not been separated from the bulk held by the defendant, so that there was no true attornment (see below). In *Maynegrain Pty. Ltd.* v. *Compafina Bank* [1982] 2 N.S.W.L.R. 141, discussed below, Hope J.A., concluded (at pp. 147–148) that even in this case the estoppel did not depend on a change of position.

Quasi-attornment

A true attornment, in the sense of one that changes constructive possession of the goods, can only occur in relation to identified goods. A bailee who purports to attorn without having earmarked goods to the claim of his new bailor is estopped from disputing that he holds goods identified to the new bailor's interest, but such estoppel confers no real rights on the bailor; it merely creates a quasi-attornment and gives the bailor a right to sue the bailee in conversion for damages if he fails to release to the bailor or his order goods of the requisite description and quantity or number.[33] This personal right is, of course, perfectly adequate so long as the bailee is solvent, but in the event of his bankruptcy the bailor is left simply with a right of proof as an unsecured creditor.[34]

Holding constructive possession for another

Can a person hold *constructive* possession of goods for another? Yes, in the sense that the other then acquires the best right to possession of the goods and can protect himself by giving notice of his rights to the bailee, who thereafter ignores those rights at his peril. But until such notice the bailee's duty is owed solely to the person for whom he has agreed to hold the goods and it is that person who has constructive possession. For example, a buyer in possession of a bill of lading deposits it with his bank, which takes delivery as pledgee. The buyer loses constructive possession of the goods, which (assuming that the bill carries any necessary indorsement) passes to the bank. The latter releases the document to the buyer against a trust receipt. The buyer now has physical possession of the bill of lading and constructive possession of the goods, but the bank has constructive possession of the bill of lading and thus the best right to possession of the goods. If the bank gives notice of this fact to the carrier the latter cannot safely release the goods to the buyer and should interplead. Similarly, if a bailee at will deposits the goods with a sub-bailee for safe keeping, the bailee holds constructive possession of the goods but since he does so for the bailor the latter has the best right to possession. Again, if a warehouse attorns to a person who is warehousing the goods as agent for an undisclosed principal, it is the agent, not the principal, who has constructive possession, but the principal has the best right to possession.

So in all these cases the person physically holding the goods continues to share possession only with the party to whom he attorned. The person ultimately entitled to possession does not, by virtue of

[33] *Hayman & Sons* v. *McLintock* 1907 S.C. 936; *Re London Wine Co. (Shippers) Ltd.* (1975), unreported, Oliver J., discussed below, p. 22, and reproduced in the Appendix, below, p. 111.
[34] *Ibid.*

that fact alone, have constructive possession, for this requires a direct attornment in his favour by the physical possessor. But the party for whose benefit constructive possession is held has the best right to possession and thus has title to sue the physical possessor for any conversion of the goods.

An illustration of this principle is to be found in the decision of the New South Wales Court of Appeal in *Maynegrain Pty. Ltd.* v. *Compafina Bank.*[35] Maynegrain held a quantity of barley in store for BTE, this being intermixed with other barley deposited by third parties. Compafina Bank had agreed with BTE to finance its purchases of barley against a pledge of the barley in store. The advances were to be made on the advice and under the control of the ANZ Banking Group acting as Compafina's agents. Maynegrain, who was unaware that ANZ was acting purely as agent, issued warehouse receipts to ANZ in which it acknowledged that the barley covered by the receipts was held for ANZ's account. Subsequently Maynegrain delivered the barley to a ship chartered by sub-purchasers, and it was found that this delivery took place without ANZ's express or implied consent. On these facts, the court held that Maynegrain's "attornment"[36] to ANZ enured for the benefit of its undisclosed principal, Compafina, who was thus entitled to sue Maynegrain for conversion of the barley.

The decision was subsequently reversed by the Privy Council[37] on the ground that ANZ knew of and assented to delivery of the barley to the ship, and that as Maynegrain was unaware of Compafina's existence as principal the question whether ANZ was acting within the scope of its actual or ostensible authority did not arise and Maynegrain was entitled to rely on ANZ's consent to the delivery. This made it unnecessary to discuss the difficult issues of law decided by the New South Wales Court of Appeal.

The reasoning of the Court of Appeal on the law is persuasive. Assuming that the act of conversion relied on was not in fact assented to by the agent, there seems no reason why the undisclosed principal should not be able to intervene and take the benefit of the estoppel in favour of his agent. Had the goods been identified and not commingled with other products, there would have been a true attornment in favour of the agent bank, and its own possession of the warehouse receipts for its principal would thus have been sufficient to give the principal not constructive possession but the right to possession of the underlying goods sufficient to ground an action for conversion.

[35] *Ibid.*

[36] Not a true attornment, since the goods were not identified, but merely an undertaking grounding an estoppel. See above, p. 11.

[37] [1984] 1 N.S.W.L.R. 389.

Loss of constructive possession

Shared possession continues only for so long as the bailee does not assert any interest of his own. Once he asserts rights over the goods, whether absolutely by defiance of the bailor's title or by asserting a limited interest such as a lien, his possession becomes exclusive and the bailor loses possession until such time as there is a fresh attornment or the bailor recovers possession in some other way. The bailor loses constructive possession, however, only if the bailee's rights are asserted over all the goods or over an identified part of them.

Exceptions to the rule that only real rights survive insolvency

There are a few cases in which the goods claimant can succeed against the owner's trustee despite the fact that he lacks a real right at the time of the bankruptcy or loses it temporarily thereafter. The first is where the bankrupt acquired the goods from the claimant through fraud, misrepresentation or other vitiating factor which entitles the claimant to rescind the contract, and he exercises that right. Since the trustee cannot stand in any better than the bankrupt, and therefore takes subject to equities, he acquires only a voidable title to the goods. Avoidance of that title by rescission of the contract revests ownership in the claimant.[38] The second case is where the goods are in the possession of a third party who holds for a temporary interest of his own and the claimant has the best right to possession when that interest has been satisfied. In this case, the claimant can assert his possessory rights against the owner's trustee even if he has not yet acquired possession at the time of the bankruptcy or, having acquired it, loses it temporarily thereafter. Two examples will illustrate this point.

Example 1

O lets goods on lease to B with permission to sub-lease to C. B grants C a sub-lease and delivers the goods to C. O then becomes insolvent. B has neither ownership nor possession. Nevertheless, he is entitled to possession, *vis-à-vis* O's trustee, on the termination of C's right to possession under the sub-lease.

Example 2

S agrees to sell to B identified goods stored in T's warehouse. B is to pay by instalments and title is not to pass to him until payment has been completed but he is given the right to immediate possession. T notifies B that in accordance with S's instructions he is holding the goods to B's order, subject, however, to satisfaction of his lien for storage charges. S then becomes bankrupt. B has neither ownership nor possession (possession is exclusively in T as the result

[38] *Re Eastgate* [1905] 1 K.B. 465; *Tilley* v. *Bowman Ltd.* [1910] 1 K.B. 745.

of his assertion of his lien), but is nevertheless entitled to the goods when T's lien has been satisfied or otherwise extinguished. The position would be the same if T had not asserted his lien until after S became bankrupt.

The point in these cases is that the trustee takes the bankrupt's property subject to any real rights in favour of a third party, including possession. So where the claimant's constructive possession follows immediately on a continuous period of possession lawfully enjoyed by one or more parties since before the bankruptcy, without any gap during which possession can have vested in the trustee, the claimant, whose title to possession *ex hypothesi* antedates the bankruptcy, has a stronger right than the trustee.

2. ACQUIRING TITLE UNDER A CONTRACT OF SALE: THE PRINCIPLES

The nature of a contract of sale

Section 2 of the Sale of Goods Act 1979, re-enacting section 1 of the Act of 1893, tells us what is meant by a contract of sale. Because of its relevance to what follows the section is worth setting out in full:

> "**2. Contract of sale**
> (1) A contract of sale of goods is a contract by which the seller transfers or agrees to transfer the property in goods to the buyer for a money consideration, called the price.
> (2) There may be a contract of sale between one part owner and another.
> (3) A contract of sale may be absolute or conditional.
> (4) Where under a contract of sale the property in the goods is transferred from the seller to the buyer the contract is called a sale.
> (5) Where under a contract of sale the transfer of the property in the goods is to take place at a future time or subject to some condition later to be fulfilled the contract is called an agreement to sell.
> (6) An agreement to sell becomes a sale when the time elapses or the conditions are fulfilled subject to which the property in the goods is to be transferred."

It should be noted that subsections (2) and (3) do not cover the case of a purported sale by a seller who neither owns nor possesses the goods. This takes effect as an agreement to sell, a point made clear by section 5(3) of the Act.

The key points in the definition of a contract of sale are that the contract relates to goods, that it involves an actual or intended transfer of ownership and that the price is payable in money. An agreement to supply and instal goods which on installation will be a fixture or otherwise part of the land or building on or in which they are incorporated will not be a contract of sale of goods if the terms of the contract are such that property will not vest in the buyer prior to installation.[39] A contract which does not involve an obligation both on the seller to sell and the buyer to buy will fall outside the statutory definition. So a hire-purchase agreement is not a contract of sale.[40] A pure barter is not a contract of sale, though the typical part-exchange transaction is, because correctly analysed it is a sale for cash in which part of the price is to be satisfied by a part-exchange allowance representing the price of the goods tendered in part-exchange under a parallel contract of sale.[41]

In most cases, it is matter of indifference whether the contract is a contract of sale or a cognate contract; but the question becomes important where the application of a provision of the Sale of Goods Act, or of some other enactment confined to sale transaction, is in issue, for if the contract is not one of sale the statutory provision will not apply.[42] Moreover, other legislation may then govern the transaction and in certain cases render it vulnerable. For example, a chattel mortgage may be disguised as a sale and letting back on lease or hire-purchase. If the court finds that the parties never genuinely intended absolute title to pass from the "seller" to the "buyer" and that the transaction was thus a sham, effect will be given to its true nature as a chattel mortgage.[43] One consequence is that if the transaction is in writing it is likely to be void for want of registration as a

[39] *Brooks Robinson Pty. Ltd.* v. *Rothfield* [1951] V.L.R. 405; *Dawber Williamson Roofing Ltd.* v. *Humberside County Council* [1979] C.L.Y. 212.

[40] *Helby* v. *Matthews* [1895] A.C. 471.

[41] *Aldridge* v. *Johnson* (1857) 7 E. & B. 885; *G.J. Dawson (Clapham) Ltd.* v. *Dutfield* [1936] 2 All E.R. 232.

[42] Thus in *Dawber Williamson Roofing Ltd.* v. *Humberside County Council*, *supra*, the plaintiffs agreed to supply and fix roofing slates under a sub-contract with the main contractors. The slates were supplied under reservation of title but were never fixed as the main contractors went into receivership and both the main contract and the sub-contract thereupon determined. The defendants, who had made a payment to the main contractors under an interim certificate covering the value of the slates brought on to the site, contended that the vesting clause in the main contract by which materials brought on to the site passed to the employer operated as a subsale which overrode the plaintiffs' title under s.25(2) of the Sale of Goods Act 1893, since the main contractors were buyers in possession within the subsection. This defence was rejected, and judgment was given for the plaintiffs, on the ground (*inter alia*) that the contract by which the plaintiffs undertook to supply and fix the slates was not a contract of sale, since at no time was it intended that title should pass to the main contractors prior to the slates becoming affixed to the roof.

[43] See, for example, *Re Watson, ex p. Official Receiver in Bankruptcy* (1890) 5 Q.B.D. 27; *Polsky* v. *S. & A. Services* [1951] 1 All E.R. 1062n; and for contrasting cases, where the transaction was upheld as genuine, *Yorkshire Railway Wagon Co.* v. *Maclure* (1882) 21 Ch.D. 309; *Staffs Motor Guarantee Ltd.* v. *British Wagon Co. Ltd.* [1934] 2 K.B. 305. See generally R. M. Goode, *Hire-Purchase Law and Practice* (2nd ed., 1970), Chap. 4.

bill of sale under the Bills of Sale Act 1878–1891 if the "seller" was an individual[44] or, in the case of a company, for want of registration under section 395 of the Companies Act 1985 as a charge created or evidenced by an instrument which would have been registrable as a bill of sale if executed by an individual.[45] Financing by sale and lease-back is now so common that the court is likely to require clear evidence of a sham before striking down a transaction.

Relevance of location of title under a contract of sale

The pivotal role of "property" in the Sale of Goods Act has long been the subject of comment. Unless otherwise agreed, the risk of loss passes to the buyer when the property is transferred to him,[46] the rules as to frustration of the contract are connected to risk[47] and thereby to property; the seller's right to the price is dependent on (*inter alia*) the transfer of the property[48]; the seller's failure to pass title results in a total failure of consideration for the buyer's price obligation, with the result that he can recover the price in full without any allowance for even a lengthy period of use of the goods[49]; and the ability of the trustee in bankruptcy of an insolvent seller or buyer to claim the goods where the insolvent party is not in possession depends in most cases on whether or not the property has passed. It is because of the important consequences flowing from the passing of property that the Act has had to lay down detailed rules as to the time when property passes "as between seller and buyer."[50] In these lectures, I shall consider some of these rules primarily in the context of their relevance when one of the parties to the contract become insolvent.

Essential prerequisites for the acquisition of title

Given that a contract between S and B is one for the sale of goods by S to B, three conditions must be satisfied before B can acquire title.

[44] See cases cited n. 43, *supra*.
[45] See Companies Act 1985, s.396(1)(c).
[46] Sale of Goods Act 1979, s.20(1).
[47] *Ibid.*, s.7.
[48] *Ibid.* s.49(1).
[49] *Rowland* v. *Divall* [1923] 2 K.B. 500.
[50] The phrase "Transfer as between seller and buyer" constituting the sub-heading to Part III of the Act has attracted both criticism (P. S. Atiyah, *The Sale of Goods* (7th ed.), p. 217) and defence (Battersby and Preston (1972) 35 M.L.R. 268). Whilst the location of title is of great importance under the Act as it stands I share Professor Atiyah's view that the need for a property concept in the Sale of Goods Act has been greatly exaggerated. For an admirable discussion of the whole topic of property and risk in a comparative context, see T. B. Smith, *Property Problems in Sale* (Tagore Law Lectures). See also Henry Ussing, "Le Transfer de la Propriété en Droit Danois" (1952) R.I.D.C. 25; Lawson & Rudden, *Law of Property* (2nd ed.), p. 232.

(1) The goods must be identified, either at the time of the contract or by some subsequent act of appropriation by one of the parties with the consent of the other.[51]
(2) The seller must either be the owner or have a power of sale.
(3) The conditions agreed by the parties, whether as to time or otherwise, for the passing of the property must have been satisfied.[52] Section 18 of the Act lays down five rules as to the presumed intention of the parties, which may be displaced by evidence of a contrary intention. A further presumption, not mentioned in section 18, is that where the seller is not merely to supply but to construct the goods ownership is not to pass until the goods have been completed. So if S agrees to build a boat for B and, having collected the price, becomes insolvent before completing the vessel, then in the absence of evidence that the property was to vest in B in the uncompleted vessel as construction proceeded S's trustee can claim the boat as an asset of S's estate,[53] whether or not it had been appropriated to the contract in its earlier stages of construction.

Even where he initially acquires title, the buyer may subsequently lose it, not only by disposing of the goods but also in a variety of other events the occurrence of any one of which will deprive him of a right to recover them.[54]

Identification

The buyer cannot acquire ownership until the goods which are to be the subject of the contract have been identified. This fundamental rule embodied in section 16 of the Act is in itself sensible enough, for how can we speak of someone as having bought goods if we cannot tell what it is that he has bought?

Where the parties identify goods at the time of the contract as being those to which the contract is to relate—as by specifying a particular car, dishwasher or painting—there is, of course, no problem. Since the agreement itself identifies its subject-matter, no subsequent act of appropriation to the contract is necessary. In the language of the Act, the contract is for the sale of specific goods.

Frequently, however, the contract is for the sale of goods that are wholly unascertained, in the sense that the contract does not identify

[51] Sale of Goods Act, ss.16, 18 rule 5(1). See below. For the effect of reservation of a right of disposal, see *ibid.*, s.19, and *The Ciudad de Pasto* [1988] 2 Lloyd's Rep. 208 and cases there cited.
[52] Sale of Goods Act 1979, ss.2(5), (6), 17, 18.
[53] *Mucklow* v. *Mangles* (1808) 1 Taunt. 318.
[54] *e.g.* where the seller remains in possession and delivers the goods to a second buyer (Sale of Goods Act, s.25); where the goods lose their identity by becoming annexed to land or buildings as a fixture or to other goods as an accession or by becoming commingled with other goods to form a new product. See *post*, pp. 71, 85, 89 *et seq.*

either particular goods or even the bulk or source of supply from which the goods are to come. For example, S agrees to sell B 100 tons of King Edward potatoes (*i.e. any* 100 tons, so long as they are King Edward) or a new 1984 Renault 9 (*i.e. any* car fitting this description). In this case, we cannot tell which are the contract potatoes, or which is the contract car, until one of the parties (usually the seller) has with the consent of the other set aside and earmarked to the contract potatoes of the given description and quantity, or a car of the given description, as the case may be. Nor, with a contract in this form, can we even point to a contractual source of supply. The seller may subsequently assert that he intended to make the supply from his factory and that the contract has been frustrated because the factory has burnt down; but to this the buyer is entitled to reply that it was not a term of the contract that the goods should be supplied from the factory, and if that source is destroyed the seller must procure the goods elsewhere. For the same reason, if the seller disposes of his entire stock of potatoes or cars to another buyer, the first buyer is not entitled to sue for conversion, for he is not in a position to say that *his* goods have been converted.

There is, however, a halfway house, though you will find no mention of it in the Sale of Goods Act. The parties may agree that the contract goods, though not precisely identified, are nevertheless to come from an identified bulk or source, *e.g.* 100 tons of grain from a total consignment of 500 tons in a warehouse, 40 1984 Renault motor cars from a consignment of 100 such cars on board an identified vessel. Though the Sale of Goods Act classifies such goods as "unascertained" in just the same way as those in the second category,[55] it is clear that they are not wholly unascertained, for we can at least say that the seller is neither entitled nor obliged to supply the goods from any other bulk or source. It follows that if the warehouse is burnt to the ground with the loss of all its contents or the ship sinks with the loss of all its cargo, the contract goods will necessarily have perished with the loss of the bulk of which they formed part, so that the seller may be able to plead frustration. Similarly, if the seller disposes of the entire bulk to another buyer, lack of precise identification of the first buyer's goods is no obstacle to a claim by him that the seller has committed the tort of conversion. I shall use the label "quasi-specific" to refer to unidentified goods which are to be supplied from an identified source.

The contract may be for the sale of quasi-specific goods from the outset or may alternatively permit or require one party to identify

[55] Contrast the case where the buyer contracts for a part interest in the entire bulk. In this case, the subject-matter of the contract is the bulk itself, not an unidentified part of it. See above, p. 2, and below, p. 21.

the source of supply subsequently, as by the seller sending the buyer a notice of appropriation identifying the vessel carrying the bulk from which the contract goods are to be supplied. I shall use the term "quasi-appropriation" to denote the post-contract identification of the source of supply.

Where the goods are identified at the time of the contract or become ascertained subsequently, one party cannot unilaterally claim the right to supply or demand different goods, even if of the same description. Similarly, where the contract is for the sale of quasi-specific goods or the source from which the contract goods are to be supplied is identified later pursuant to the contract, it is not open to seller or buyer to change the source of supply without the other's consent. However, if for any reason an appropriation or quasi-appropriation proves ineffective, as where the nominated vessel carrying the goods fails to sail or where the buyer exercises a right to reject ascertained goods as not in conformity with the contract description, it is open to the appropriating party to make a fresh appropriation, provided that he is still in time to do so.[56]

Appropriation not necessarily coincident with passing of property

It is important not to fall into the trap of assuming that appropriation automatically transfers ownership to the buyer. Appropriation as such does no more than identify the contract goods. Whether the property in them is to pass to the buyer on such appropriation or at a later stage depends on the intention of the parties.

3. *ACQUIRING TITLE: SOME PRACTICAL PROBLEMS*

What constitutes a sufficient act of appropriation

To be effective, the appropriation must be unconditional and must be done either by the seller with the buyer's consent or by the buyer with the seller's consent.[57] An example of the latter is where, pursuant to the contract, the buyer helps himself from the seller's stock to the given contract quantity. Assent to appropriation may be given in advance of the act of appropriation, but unless that act is one which puts the goods outside the seller's control (*e.g.* by delivering them to an independent carrier consigned to the buyer) or is an act expressly called for by the contract (*e.g.* a notice of appropriation) it is usually extremely difficult to show that the act in question represents an irrevocable decision to appropriate rather than an act

[56] *Borrowman Phillips & Co.* v. *Free & Hollis* (1878) 4 Q.B.D. 500; *E.E. & Brian Smith (1928) Ltd.* v. *Wheatsheaf Mills Ltd.* [1939] 2 K.B. 302; *McDougall* v. *Aeromarine of Emsworth Ltd.* [1958] 1 All E.R. 431.

[57] Sale of Goods Act, s.18, rule 5(1).

of indoor management which the party performing it may feel free to undo at pleasure.[58] Two examples will illustrate the difficulty:

Example 1

S, having agreed to sell B six cases of wine from S's cellars, instructs his storeman to label six cases with B's name and address. Unless S informs B of this labelling and B assents, or B had previously agreed with S that the first act of labelling in B's name was to constitute an appropriation to the contract, the court is likely to find that the labelling by S's storeman was merely an act of indoor management and was not intended by S to prevent him from changing his mind and having the name on the labels changed to that of another customer whose needs were more pressing.

Example 2

S agrees to make a car for B in accordance with a design and specification which B has seen and approved. It is agreed that ownership shall vest in B when the car is completed. S collects most of the price in advance, constructs a car in accordance with the design and specification and then becomes bankrupt before B has seen the car. In the absence of evidence that with the knowledge and assent of B it was S's intention to appropriate the car to the contract, it forms part of S's estate, for S may well have decided to make a similar car for himself or for another customer and to construct a separate vehicle for B.[59] The position would no doubt be otherwise if the design and specifications had been furnished by B, for S would then have been precluded from using them for his own benefit, or for that of another customer, without B's consent, so that his intention to appropriate the car to the contract could be assumed.

The most usual form of unconditional appropriation is the performance of an act by which the seller loses control of the goods. The obvious case is delivery direct to the buyer; but delivery of the goods to an independent carrier consigned to the buyer is equally effective, though the position is otherwise if the seller consigns the goods to his own order with the intention of reserving a right of disposal.[60] Another way in which the seller can divest himself of control is by delivering to the buyer the document of title relating to the goods.

[58] *Healy* v. *Howlett & Sons* [1917] 1 K.B. 337; *Carlos Federspiel & Co. S.A.* v. *Charles Twigg & Co. Ltd.* [1957] 1 Lloyd's Rep. 240.

[59] In the words of Heath J., in *Mucklow* v. *Mangles* (1808) 1 Taunt. 318 at p. 319: "A tradesman often finishes goods, which he is making in pursuance of an order given by one person, and sells them to another." This comment was made to illustrate a somewhat different point, namely the presumed intention of the parties that ownership of goods to be made is not to pass until they have been completed, but it is equally opposite to the issue of appropriation.

[60] Sale of Goods Act, s.19(1), (2).

Sale of an unidentified part of a bulk held by seller

S, a wine merchant, has 100 bottles of wine in his cellar. He contracts to sell 99 bottles to B, collects the price and agrees to hold the bottles for B until required. S then becomes bankrupt without having delivered any of the bottles to B or appropriated any bottles to the contract. In this situation, B has no proprietary claim to a single bottle, for it cannot be said of any one bottle that it is not the bottle excluded from the purchase. But if, before becoming bankrupt, S had delivered one bottle to a friend or buyer, or if one bottle had rolled off the shelf and smashed, B's 99 bottles would become ascertained by exhaustion,[61] with the result that he could claim them from the trustee or liquidator.[62]

The position is similar where S sells 20 bottles out of 100 bottles to each of five buyers, but does not deliver or otherwise appropriate any bottle to any of the contracts. At that stage, no buyer has any possessory or proprietary rights, for although S has in effect contracted to sell his entire stock, each sale is of an unascertained part of that stock. Accordingly we cannot simply aggregate the purchases and say that the purchasers are tenants in common in equal shares. They are simply unsecured creditors.[63]

But suppose we vary the terms of the two contracts slightly, so that what B agrees to buy in the first contract is not 99 bottles of wine but a 99 per cent. share of the contents of S's wine cellar; and that what each buyer agrees to buy under the second set of contracts is not 20 bottles but a 20 per cent. share of the total stock. Now the position is entirely different. The effect of the first contract is that B and S become tenants in common of the entire quantity in the proportion 99:1, so that if S becomes insolvent B can claim his 99 per cent. and S's creditors must content themselves with the remaining one per cent.; whilst under the second set of contracts, each sale results in the seller transferring a 20 per cent. share in his stock to the buyer, so that after the fifth sale the seller has no remaining interest and the five buyers are tenants in common in equal shares.[64] This would also be the position, of course, if all five buyers clubbed together at the outset and agreed to purchase the entire stock together as tenants in common—or, if they preferred, as joint tenants.[65]

[61] *Wait & James* v. *Midland Bank Ltd.* (1926) 31 Com.Cas. 172; *Karlshamns Olijefabrike* v. *Eastport Navigation Corp.* [1982] 3 All E.R. 208.

[62] Assuming that any other conditions necessary for the transfer of ownership have been satisfied.

[63] *Re London Wine Co. (Shippers) Ltd.*, (1975), unreported, Oliver J. See below, pp. 22, 111.

[64] Not joint tenants, because *ex hypothesi* the purchases take place at different times, so that the unity of time required for a joint tenancy is lacking. However, the tenancy in common takes effect at law, not merely in equity. See above, p. 6.

[65] See above, p. 6.

Sale of an unascertained part of a bulk held by warehouse or carrier

Exactly the same principle applies where the bulk is held not by the seller but by his bailee, typically in a warehouse or on board a ship. S agrees to sell to B 99 of the 100 cases of wine held for S by W in W's warehouse. Until the 99 cases have been set aside by S or W and appropriated to the contract, B has no proprietary rights in any of the wine. Now let us suppose that S contracts to sell to B the whole of the wine held for S in W's warehouse but that this itself forms only part of a larger quantity of such wine in the warehouse, and W has not irrevocably set aside the cases he is holding for S. Since S's own interest in the warehouse stock is still only quasi-specific, he cannot transfer an interest in specific cases to B, even by agreeing to sell to B the full number of cases to which he, S, is entitled. This is a point which some sellers quite genuinely fail to appreciate, with the result that they inform their buyers in all good faith that each such buyer is now the owner of a given number of cases of wine in the warehouse, and may even issue, or procure W to issue, to each buyer a so-called certificate of title or warehouse receipt which is expressed to be transferable by delivery. All of which achieves, in proprietary terms, precisely nothing!

A bibulous illustration—the case of the London Wine Company

The principles formulated above are not mere theoretical abstractions. They were actually invoked, and very thoroughly analysed, in *Re London Wine Co. (Shippers) Ltd.*,[66] in which Oliver J. (as he then was) gave a detailed and highly illuminating judgment which unaccountably failed to reach the law reports. The case is notable for the skill with which different counsel representing the various buyers sought, albeit unsuccessfully, to persuade the court that lack of precise identification was not a barrier to a proprietary claim; and as you will by now have guessed, it concerned the sale of large numbers of cases of wine in a warehouse! The facts are worth setting out in some detail, because they provide a moral for those who buy wine and lay them down in an independent warehouse, or in the cellars of a wine merchant, without visiting the premises from time to time to see that their purchases have been duly labelled.

The company in liquidation (or, as my local newspaper happily put it, in liquidisation) was a wine dealer who acquired substantial stocks of wine which had been deposited in various warehouses. The company issued a brochure entitled "Claret Investment. How it works and why." This explained that intending investors could buy wine from the company by the dozen, lying in bond, and that each

[66] (1975), unreported, Oliver J., reproduced in the Appendix, *post*, pp. 111 *et seq.*

buyer would receive (as indeed he did) a certificate from the company or direct from the warehouse establishing that he was the beneficial owner of the wine. Each certificate would contain a description of the wine and the number of cases held for the buyer in the warehouse. A buyer might wish to sell his wine or pledge it to his bank. In that event, he would be asked to surrender his certificate of title, and a fresh certificate would be issued to the new buyer or, in the case of a pledge to the bank, the warehouse would confirm to the bank that it was holding the pledgor's wine to the bank's order. However, no wine was segregated until delivery, segregation being considered impracticable for the warehouse operation. The case involved three types of transaction. In the first, a single buyer purchased what amounted to the total of the company's stock stated to be "lying in bond," no warehouse being specified. In the second, there were a number of purchasers of wine whose purchases together exhausted the whole of the company's stocks of wine held in different warehouses. In the third, there were a number of purchasers, but their acquisitions did not exhaust the company's stocks, and a bank to whom one of them had mortgaged his wine was given an acknowledgment by the warehouse that the appropriate quantity of wine was held to its order. The total stocks held by the warehouses in question were more than sufficient to meet the claims of all the purchasers, so that there was no competition among the purchasers. The matter came before the court because, the wine company having defaulted under its debenture given to its bank, the bank appointed a receiver who sought the court's directions as to the disposition of the wine stocks. None of the warehouses involved was a party to the application.

The following arguments were advanced on behalf of one buyer or another:

(1) In the first transaction, where the contract of sale did not identify the warehouse but the quantity sold accounted for the entirety of the company's stock held at the warehouse where it was stored, it was argued that the goods had become ascertained by exhaustion, so that section 16 was satisfied. This was rejected—and *Wait & James* v. *Midland Bank Ltd.*[67] distinguished—on the ground that the warehouse was not specified as the contractual source of supply, so that whilst the wine company may have intended to appropriate its entire stock in that warehouse to the order, it could equally well have supplied from another source.

(2) Alternatively, the stock belonging to the company in the warehouse became held on trust for the buyers. This argument failed on the ground that one could not have a trust of

[67] See n. 61, above.

unidentified property.[68] Just as it was not sufficient for the purpose of section 16 of the Sale of Goods Act that the company owned a stock of wine *capable* of being used as the source of supply, if it was not contractually designated as such, so also the fact that the company intended to confer a beneficial interest on a purchaser by way of trust and had stock available for that purpose did not suffice to constitute a trust in the absence of evidence that such stock had in fact been earmarked for the trust. Moreover, even if the mass itself were identifiable, a statement that a particular buyer was the sole and beneficial owner of, say, 10 cases of wine could not be construed as giving him by way of trust a beneficial interest in such part of the mass as 10 cases bore to the total number of cases comprising the mass. In short, as in the case of sale, one could not have a trust of unascertained or quasi-specific goods.

(3) As a further alternative, the company's contractual obligation to supply a given number of cases of wine to the buyer constituted an equitable assignment of that quantity out of the stock owned by the company. The learned judge treated this argument as essentially a repetition of the trust argument in a different guise and rejected it on similar grounds, adopting a passage from the judgment of Atkin L.J., in *Re Wait*[69] that whilst an agreement to make a present transfer of property passed the beneficial ownership at once and entitled the transferee to specific performance, it did not logically follow that whenever there was a contract of which a court of equity would decree specific performance, the beneficial interest had passed. It was necessary for the subject-matter to be ascertained.

(4) Next, the buyer had a right to specific performance of the contract to sell him a given number of cases of wine, and the bank acquired its charge over the stock subject to the buyer's right to specific performance. This was rejected on two counts. First, the power to award specific performance under section 52 of the Sale of Goods Act was confined to specific or ascertained goods, and the decision of the Court of Appeal in *Re Wait*[70] was a serious obstacle to the contention that independently of section 52 the court had a general equitable power to decree specific performance of a contract for the sale of unascertained goods. Secondly, even if specific performance of such a contract could be decreed, the decree would

[68] Citing *Re Wait* [1927] 1 Ch. 606.
[69] *Ibid.*, at p. 634.
[70] *Ibid.*

not relate to specific goods and accordingly could not confer on the buyer priority over the bank's charge.

(5) Finally, the company, having represented to the buyer that he had become the owner of a given number of cases of wine, was estopped from denying that it had appropriated particular cases of wine to the contract, and the bank as chargee was bound by that estoppel. This contention was no more successful than the others. If the goods were not ascertained, the buyer could not acquire proprietary rights by estoppel; he had at most a personal claim against the company for conversion.[71]

The case is a graphic illustration of the risks run by a buyer who purchases, or a bank which lends on the security of, an unidentified part of a bulk and leaves it in storage in the hands of the seller or of a third party without ensuring its segregation and appropriation to the purchase or security interest.

Is the law satisfactory?

We have seen that whereas a contract to sell 99 bottles out of 100 held in store by the seller or his bailee confers no proprietary interest in the buyer until appropriation, the sale of a 99 per cent. share of the total quantity held in store would (assuming ownership was intended to pass without delay or other condition) make the buyer a tenant in common with the seller in the proportion 99:1, and that accordingly if different buyers purchased different percentages of the total stock they would become tenants in common in the proportion of their respective interests. So by using the right incantation when doing the deal, a buyer can transform his position. Section 16 of the Act is no longer a problem (even if we assume that the contract is within the Act, which is not entirely clear[72]), because in this form the contract relates to a proportionate interest in the entire bulk, so that the contract goods *are* ascertained for the purpose of section 16.

It is surely unreasonable that so much should be made to turn on the niceties of a verbal formulation. The real question is one of policy: who should have priority in S's insolvency, B or the general body of creditors? The draftsmen of the Uniform Commercial Code were in no doubt that B should be recognized as having an interest in common whichever formulation was adopted:

> "An undivided share in an identified bulk of fungible goods is sufficiently identified to be sold although the quantity of the

[71] See above, p. 11.

[72] Under s.2(2) there may be a contract of sale between one part owner and another but the subsection does not expressly cover the case of sale by an owner of part of his interest. See R. M. Goode, *Commercial Law*, (1985) pp. 157–158; Benjamin's *Sale of Goods* (3rd ed.), para. 119.

bulk is not determined. An agreed proportion of such a bulk or any quantity thereof agreed upon by number, weight or other measure may to the extent of the seller's interest in the bulk be sold to the buyer who then becomes an owner in common."[73]

With this must be read sections 2–502 and 7–207 of the Code. The former gives the buyer who has paid part or all of the price a special property in the goods, and a right to recover them from the seller on tender of any unpaid balance, if the seller becomes insolvent within ten days after receipt of the first instalment. The latter requires a warehouseman to keep non-fungibles separate so as to permit at all times identification and delivery, and provides that commingled fungibles are owned in common by the persons entitled thereto and the warehouseman is severally liable to each owner for that owner's share. Taken together, these provisions reflect the view of the Code that the creditors of the seller or the warehouse would be given an unjustified windfall if they were allowed to rely on traditional property concepts to defeat the claim of a buyer to an undivided interest in an identified bulk.[74]

English law has yet to formulate a coherent policy on the treatment of conflicting claims in insolvency; but that is a subject for another day!

[73] s.2–105(4).

[74] See also R. M. Goode, "Ownership and Obligation in Commercial Transactions" (1987) 103 L.Q.R. 433 at pp. 447 *et seq.*

II

Acquiring Title to Oil, Gas and Minerals

The acquisition of title to minerals[1] and petroleum products[2] raises many of the conceptual issues discussed in my first lecture: in particular, those relating to the identification of the subject-matter, the distinction between contract and property rights, the exercise of effective control and the incidents of co-ownership. But the very nature of these objects of purchase poses a whole range of very distinct questions. Does their fugacious character[3] preclude them from being the subject of ownership at all before being reduced to possession?[4] What is the legal nature of a right to extract petroleum and minerals? Can they be the subject of sale prior to extraction? To what extent have the common law rights of the landowner been cut down by statute? And in the case of oil below the United Kingdom continental shelf but outside territorial waters, who owns the rights of exploration and exploitation, how does property become vested in a licensee and how are joint interests or undivided interests in common converted through appropriation into interests *in specie*? Finally, what law governs these issues?

In this one lecture I cannot hope to do more than set out some general principles, pinpoint various problems and offer what are sometimes tentative conclusions. For those who wish to pursue the subject in detail, I can warmly commend the looseleaf work *United Kingdom Oil and Gas Law*, by Professor Terence Daintith and Mr. Geoffrey Willoughby, which I have found an invaluable guide. Other very helpful works are volumes 31 and 35 of Halsbury's

[1] The word "mineral" has no primary or literal meaning (*Caledonian Rly. Co.* v. *Glenboig Union Fireclay Co.* [1911] A.C. 290; *Earl of Lonsdale* v. *Attorney-General* [1982] 3 All E.R. 579) and depending on its context may cover all or anything recoverable from the earth by mining, whether organic or inorganic and whether solid, liquid or gaseous. In popular parlance it is usually confined to inorganic solids. Various statutes have prescribed different definitions. See *Halsbury's Laws* (4th ed.), vol. 31, paras. 8 *et seq.*

[2] Similarly, the terms "petroleum" and "petroleum products" have no definite meaning at common law (*Borys* v. *Canadian Pacific Rly. Co.* [1953] A.C. 217), though again there are various statutory definitions. See, for example, the Petroleum (Production) Act 1934, s.1(2), and other legislation referred to in *Halsbury's Laws* (4th ed.), Vol. 35, para. 1202 and Supplement.

[3] Fugacious: having a tendency to escape or evaporate; volatile; transitory; hard to capture or keep.

[4] As in the case of flowing water, which at common law is incapable of ownership.

Laws[5] and an excellent Australian work, *Australian Mining and Petroleum Laws* (2nd ed.), by Dr. John Forbes and Mr. Andrew Lang, which also contains useful material on the English common law.

My concern to-night is with issues of ownership and control arising from the extraction of petroleum and minerals and, in the case of offshore extraction, their conveyance to ship or shore. Dealings in oil in transit by traders in the commodity markets, and the problems caused by delay in the arrival of bills of lading, will be dealt with in my next lecture.

1. *OWNERSHIP IN GENERAL*

I shall begin by describing the general common law principles governing the ownership of petroleum and minerals and then consider the complex network of legislation that has to a very considerable degree destroyed original private ownership of these products. This will be followed by an examination of the legal issues arising from the extraction of offshore petroleum, with particular reference to questions of ownership, risk and security rights.

(1) The Common Law

Surface owner owns sub-surface materials

The presumption at common law is that whoever owns the surface of the land owns the soil, minerals and other things lying beneath it.[6] This is expressed in the old maxim *cujus est solum, ejus est usque ad coelum et ad inferos*, though with the advent of aircraft, space missiles and satellites this statement of the common law position has become recognised as just a shade too extravagant! Whether oil and gas, being fugacious, were at common law susceptible of ownership before being captured remains a matter of debate.[7] I need not spend time on it, because the nationalisation of all petroleum in its natural

[5] Titles "Mines," "Minerals and Quarries" and "Petroleum Production" respectively.

[6] *Pountney* v. *Clayton* (1883) 11 Q.B.D. 820; *Commissioner of Railways* v. *Valuer-General* [1974] A.C. 328.

[7] There is no English decision directly in point. In the United States, two rival theories have developed. The first is the "non-ownership" theory adopted by states such as Oklahoma, Louisiana and California, which holds that oil, like wild animals, is not susceptible to ownership until reduced to possession. The second, adopted by several states, including Texas and Kansas, is the "ownership in place" theory, under which oil beneath land belongs to the landowner as part of the soil but the landowner's interest is defeasible, being lost if the oil migrates to the land of another. See Williams & Meyers, *Oil and Gas Law*, Chap. 2; John S. Lowe, *Oil and Gas Law*, pp. 8–12, 22–24. Both theories predicate that a landowner cannot incur any liability for extracting oil that has migrated to his land from that of another,

condition in strata[8] has made the issue academic. Accordingly in what immediately follows I shall confine my remarks to minerals, which, with the exception of coal and royal metals, can continue in private ownership.

Grant of rights over sub-surface minerals

The owner of the surface land may grant rights in or to the underlying minerals at common law. This may be done in one of two ways. First, since ownership of land may be divided horizontally or vertically in any way the owner and his transferee agree, the owner may sell an identified stratum of land in which the minerals are located, *e.g.* the stratum commencing 100 feet and ending 200 feet below the surface; and different strata may be sold to different purchasers. Secondly, the surface owner may grant a *profit à prendre* to another to extract and carry away minerals from beneath the owner's land. Such a *profit à prendre* may be granted in gross or as part of a mining lease or licence of the relevant stratum.[9] If granted for an interest equivalent to an estate in fee simple or a term of years absolute, the *profit à prendre* constitutes a legal interest in land, otherwise it takes effect as an equitable interest.[10] The grantee of the interest is not an estate owner; the interest he acquires is a *jus in re aliena*, a right in another's property. From the viewpoint of the surface owner, a *profit à prendre* is a servitude. The sale of a stratum or grant of a *profit à prendre* carries with it by implication a right to get and carry away the minerals, even if this involves digging or cutting through the surface land or through strata retained by the surface owner, so long as no permanent damage or destruction is caused[11] and the surface is properly supported.[12]

Until extraction the minerals constitute part of the land and cannot be the subject of a sale or other disposition *in situ*. Only by abstraction from the soil (whether at the surface or through a constructed well, shaft, etc.) do they acquire the status of chattels.[13]

and in view of the virtual impossibility of establishing the source of oil *in situ* it seems almost certain that English law would have adopted the same approach had not nationalisation of petroleum made the whole issue theoretical.

[8] Petroleum (Production) Act 1934, s.1, as amended by Oil and Gas (Enterprise) Act 1982, s.18(1).

[9] *Wilkinson* v. *Proud* (1843) 11 M. & W. 43; *Gowan* v. *Christie* (1873) L.R. 2 Sc. & Div. 273; Forbes and Lang, *Australian Mining and Petroleum Laws* (2nd ed.), Chap. 2.

[10] Law of Property Act 1925, s.1(2)(*a*).

[11] *Earl of Cardigan* v. *Armitage* (1823) 2 B. & C. 197.

[12] *Humphreys* v. *Brogden* (1850) 2 Q.B. 739; *Rowbotham* v. *Wilson* (1860) 8 H.L. Cas. 348.

[13] *Port* v. *Turton* (1763) 2 Wils. 169; *Wilkinson* v. *Proud*, *supra*; Law of Property Act 1925, s.205(1)(ix).

No private ownership of royal metals

All gold and silver in gold and silver mines is vested in the Crown by virtue of the royal prerogative,[14] as relaxed by statute.[15]

Rights in the sea-shore

The owner of land adjoining the sea is entitled to the sea-shore down to the medium-high water mark, and all that lies beneath it, but the foreshore (*i.e.* the ground between the medium-high and low water marks) belongs to the Crown.[16]

Rights in the United Kingdom Continental Shelf

Apart from legislation,[17] rights in the United Kingdom Continental Shelf[18] are governed by customary and conventional international law, under which the United Kingdom has sovereign rights of exploration and exploitation of the sea bed, subsoil and their natural resources to the outer edge of the continental margin;[19] but the U.K.C.S. does not constitute part of the territory of the United Kingdom.[20]

[14] *The Case of Mines* (1565) 1 Plowd. 310.

[15] Royal Mines Acts 1688 and 1693; *Att.-Gen.* v. *Morgan* [1891] 1 Ch. 432.

[16] *Att.-Gen.* v. *Chambers* (1854) 4 De G. M. & G. 206; *Att.-Gen.* v. *Emerson* [1891] A.C. 469.

[17] Continental Shelf Act 1964, s.1 and Orders in Council made thereunder. See below.

[18] In the geomorphological sense, the continental shelf is the gently sloping gradient adjacent to the continental land mass. The concept of the continental shelf in international law is much broader. The shelf is considered to start at the outer limit of the coastal state's territorial sea and to encompass not only the shelf proper but the continental slope (the sharp slope falling away from the edge of the shelf) and the continental rise (a more gradual slope linking the base of the continental slope to the deep sea-bed. The shelf, the slope and the rise together constitute the continental margin. See generally R. W. Bentham, "The Concept of a Continental Shelf and the Financial Problems of Exploitation," *Fifth Commonwealth Law Conference Proceedings and Papers* (1977) at p. 439.

[19] See the Convention on the Law of the Sea 1982, art. 76, which represents the best statement of present customary international law on the concept of the continental shelf. However, the U.K. has not yet become a party to this Convention, and its rights under conventional law remain those set out in the Geneva Convention on the Continental Shelf 1958.

[20] The exact nature of the U.K.'s rights in its continental shelf has never been precisely defined. For contrasting views, see P. Marriage, "North Sea Petroleum Project Financing in the United Kingdom," 5 Int'l Bus. Lawyer 207, 216–217 (1977), who considers that the Crown's rights are purely regulatory, and Daintith and Willoughby, who consider that they are proprietary (*United Kingdom Oil and Gas Law*, para. 1–204), and are supported in this by Lewis and Willoughby, "Production Payments in the United Kingdom," 3 Hous. J. Int'l L. 51, 57 (1980).

Coal and coal mines

All interests in unworked coal and coal mines and of collieries in minerals that can only be worked economically in association with coal are now vested in the National Coal Board,[21] together with any rights exercisable by the United Kingdom over U.K.C.S. coal.[22]

Petroleum

All petroleum (including oil and natural gas) existing in its natural condition in strata in Great Britain or beneath the territorial waters of the United Kingdom[23] is vested in the Crown, together with the exclusive right to search and bore for and get the petroleum.[24] Further, by the Continental Shelf Act 1964, s.1, any rights exercisable by the United Kingdom outside territorial waters with respect to the sea bed and subsoil and their natural resources are vested in the Crown or, in the case of coal, the National Coal Board.[25] The effect of this provision is to incorporate into domestic law the rules of customary and conventional international law concerning the Continental Shelf, including the principles previously mentioned.

2. EXTRACTION OF OFFSHORE PETROLEUM

The applicable law

The legal analysis that follows in relation to the extraction of offshore petroleum is confined to England and assumes that English law is applicable to determine the rights of the parties. However, in

[21] Coal Act 1938; Coal Industry Nationalisation Act 1946, s.5, and Sched. 1, para. 1; Opencast Coal Act 1958, ss.9, 39; Mines (Working Facilities and Support) Act 1966.

[22] Continental Shelf Act 1964, s.1.

[23] The reference to the territorial waters was inserted into section 1 of the Petroleum (Production) Act 1934 by s.18(2) of the Oil and Gas (Enterprise) Act 1982 as the result of the dictum by Slade J. in *Earl of Lonsdale* v. *Attorney-General* [1982] 3 All E.R. 579 that the words "Great Britain" in s.1 of the former Act did not include territorial waters. The amendment introduced by the 1982 Order embodied the phrase "territorial waters of the United Kingdom adjacent to Great Britain" but s.1 was further amended to delete the words "adjacent to Great Britain" so as to encompass the territorial waters of Northern Ireland (Petroleum Act 1987, s.19 and Sched. 3). The territorial sea adjacent to the United Kingdom was extended from 3 to 12 nautical miles by s.1 of the Territorial Sea Act 1987 except with respect to the vesting of rights in coal under s.1(2) of the Continental Shelf Act 1964 (Territorial Sea Act 1987, s.2(3)).

[24] Petroleum (Production) Act 1934, s.1(1), (2).

[25] Areas in which such rights are exercisable are designated by Orders in Council under s.1(7) of the Continental Shelf Act 1964.

many cases this will not be so. The Civil Jurisdiction (Offshore Activities) Order 1987 (which replaced the Continental Shelf (Jurisdiction) Order 1980) divides the U.K.C.S. into three areas, the English area, the Scottish area and the Northern Irish area. English law governs the determination of questions arising out of acts or omissions taking place in the English area, in connection with the exploration of the sea bed or subsoil or the exploitation of their natural resources, and Scottish or Northern Irish law governs such questions where they arise out of acts or omissions taking place in the Scottish or Northern Irish area, as the case may be.[26]

The scope of these provisions is unclear.[27] They appear wide enough to cover claims in both tort and contract arising from acts or omissions in the designated area. In the case of a claim in contract the reference to English law would, it is thought, include its conflict of laws rules, thus subjecting the contract to its proper law as ascertained in accordance with the conflict of laws.[28] However, it may not always be easy to determine whether an act or omission takes place "in connection with the exploration of the sea bed or subsoil or the exploitation of their natural resources." Is this confined to claims or defences based directly on such acts or omissions or might the provisions extend to supply and security agreements which provide for the transfer of, or the grant of a security interest in, oil or gas produced by boring and extraction in the U.K.C.S.? In practice, the problem is unlikely to arise in most cases, either because the relevant contract will contain an express choice of law clause or because there is likely to be a sufficiently close connection with England, Scotland or Northern Ireland to leave no doubt that its law is applicable under normal conflict of laws rules.

Physical features

Though commonly used to denote a liquid (crude oil) found underground in sedimentary rocks, petroleum in its broad sense encompasses all hydrocarbon mixtures in the earth, whether in gaseous, liquid or solid form or as a gas in solution. Petroleum is classified as being from light to heavy, depending on the length of its carbon chain. The lightest forms, containing one and two carbon atoms respectively, are methane and ethane, natural gases which may be found either dry or in solution. Liquid petroleum ranges from light oils such as propane, butane and natural gasolene, to heavy crude, such as bitumen. Though natural gas may exist in completely dry form, *i.e.* unassociated with oil, all liquid petroleum

[26] Civil Jurisdiction (Offshore Activities) Order 1987, made under s.23 of the Oil and Gas (Enterprises) Act 1982.
[27] Daintith and Willoughby *op. cit.* n. 20, above, paras. 1–237 *et seq.*
[28] *Ibid.* para. 1–238.

contains some gas, the ratio of gas to oil increasing with increased pressure, temperature and depth of burial.

Where one or more reservoirs, or pools, of petroleum are trapped within a defined geological rock structure, the area encompassed by that structure is known as a field. For commercial purposes there are three principal types of field, namely: an ordinary crude oil field, with no more than a little gas in solution; a condensate field, in which a substantial amount of gas is mixed with oil; and a dry gas field, in which there is almost no liquid. Gas from a dry gas field is extracted in gaseous form and kept so under pressure until landed. Gas in a condensate field is either separated out for commercial use or, if this is uneconomic, disposed of by flaring, for which the consent of the Secretary of State is required.[29]

Transportation of petroleum

After pumping, the petroleum is treated at the well-head for impurities. It then has to be brought ashore. Crude oil is either piped to a shore terminal, in which case the gas can safely be left in it until it has been landed, or piped from the platform to a loading buoy, or spar, and thence to a tanker, in which event the gas must for safety reasons be separated out at the platform and either brought ashore separately or flared. Dry gas is piped in gaseous form from the platform to the shore and then liquified and placed in storage tanks or a gas ship.

Licensing

Though the U.K.C.S. does not form part of United Kingdom territory, the United Kingdom has under international law exclusive rights of exploration and exploitation, including the right to exclude others,[30] so that even if it lacks full ownership it undoubtedly has rights of a proprietary nature which enable it to exclude or restrict exploration and production by private enterprise. A person wishing to explore and extract petroleum from beneath the U.K.C.S is required to obtain seaward exploration and production licences under the Petroleum (Production) (Seaward Areas) Regulations 1988. Periodically the Secretary of State announces a new licensing round and invites interested parties to bid for licences for designated blocks or parts thereof. Though it is open to a single enterprise to apply for a licence, the size of each project is such that nowadays each application is almost invariably made by a number of companies acting in concert, and on a successful application the licence is granted to the applicants jointly. The licence sets out a description

[29] See cl. 21(3)–(7) of the model clauses embodied in Schedule 5 to the Petroleum (Production) Regulations 1976.

[30] Geneva Convention on the Continental Shelf 1958, Pt. 2.

of the licensed area by reference to stated co-ordinates, prescribes the royalties to be paid and incorporates by reference such of the model clauses set out in regulations[31] as are considered appropriate. The model clauses empower the Secretary of State to revoke the licence in a variety of events, and in particular enable him to revoke it for default without giving the licensee an opportunity to remedy the breach.

Nature and assignability of licence

The production licence is an exclusive licence to search and bore for, and get, petroleum in the sea bed and subsoil under the designated seaward area. The legal character of the licence has never been determined but the closest analogy is with the domestic *profit à prendre*.[32] However, since the Law of Property Act is confined to England and Wales,[33] the licence cannot confer a legal interest in the sea bed and subsoil. Indeed, since the Crown's own rights in the U.K.C.S. are not those of a full owner it is doubtful whether a licence amounts to more than an exclusive personal right to bore for and get petroleum.

The successful applicants for each licence are referred to in the licence collectively as "the licensee." Accordingly they are joint holders of the licence at law,[34] but since the joint operating agreement which governs their relationship invariably provides for the parties to be undivided owners of the licence in differing percentages, and for royalties and other payments to be borne in proportion to the parties' respective interests, the parties are in equity tenants in common of the licence in the percentages agreed.

Subject to the consent of the Secretary of State, and to the terms of the agreement between the participants, an interest in common in a licence is freely transferable, and licence interests are indeed frequently assigned or charged to a bank by way of security.[35]

Operating arrangements

The participants who together constitute the licensee enter into a detailed Joint Operating Agreement setting out their respective rights and duties. This will provide for the appointment of one of the parties as operator to conduct operations under the agreement. The operator's duties will include assembly of the project team, maintenance of records of petroleum extracted, quantities lifted by each par-

[31] See n. 29, above.
[32] See above, p. 29.
[33] Law of Property Act 1925, s.209(3).
[34] A legal tenancy in common, though capable of subsisting in goods, is not possible in the case of choses in action (*Re McKerrell* [1912] 2 Ch. 648, *per* Joyce J. at p. 653), and this principle would apply to rights under a licence.
[35] But see *post*, p. 37.

ticipant, incomes and expenditures, and the like, and empower the operator to make cash calls on the participants to meet the project expenses as these are incurred. Policies will be laid down by an Operating Committee, and the operator will work within the Committee's guidelines.

Unitisation and re-unitisation

It not infrequently happens that two or more blocks licensed to different licensees lie within the same geological field. In such a case it may be necessary for the two groups of licensees to work the field together as a whole—indeed, this is insisted upon by the Secretary of State where so required to achieve maximum economic recovery and avoid competitive drilling—to prevent activities in one block leading to the draining of oil or gas from the other, to the detriment of the licensees of the latter and of efficient working of the field. There may also be unitisation across boundaries, as where one field straddles the United Kingdom and Norwegian sectors. Since the structure of the field is not fully known at the outset, and the parties' perception of what constitutes the field changes as they acquire more knowledge of the blocks they are working, there is a periodic re-unitisation to match the newly discovered physical conditions.

Commingling and separation of petroleum

(1) *Ownership*

As previously stated, English law does not recognize separate ownership of petroleum *in situ*, so that ownership rights in offshore oil will not be acquired until the oil has been captured. This would seem to be when it enters the operator's well, thus becoming separated from the natural subsoil. At that point it will be owned by the participants in common, and they in turn may be co-owners with another group with whom they are jointly working a different block in the same field under a unitisation agreement.

The point at which separation into the individual interests takes place depends on the circumstances. The individual participants make nominations to receive lifts of oil or gas in an agreed sequence, under the overall control of the operator. Appropriation is made, and single ownership is acquired, by a party at the time he makes a lift. Where crude oil is piped on to a tanker furnished by one of the participants, then under the standard transfer of property clause ownership of the oil passes to the participant at the point where it passes the flange between the loading hose and the tanker's cargo valve. Similarly, where the oil is piped ashore and transferred into a participant's tank, property is generally expressed to pass when the oil crosses the permanent hose connection at the storage point. Until then, the oil, whether held at the platform, in a spar or in the pipeline, continues in common ownership. The position with gas is rather different. Almost all gas is supplied to British Gas plc, which concludes separate long-term supply agreements with each participant. However, the gas is piped ashore direct into the British Gas storage facilities without ever being split up among the participants. Indeed, the gas from different fields may well be commingled in the same pipeline. Hence what British Gas receives is an undivided stream of gas under a number of contracts with different participants, each contract being simultaneously performed by the transfer of the particular participant's interest in common in the stream. Presumably this aggregation of undivided interests results in British Gas acquiring legal title to the whole stream at the point where it passes into the company's possession.

(2) *Risk*

Unless otherwise agreed, this passes with the property.[36] However, where control of an undivided part of a bulk passes from seller to buyer, the court will ordinarily infer an agreement that the risk is to pass also. A good illustration is the case of *Sterns Ltd.* v. *Vickers.*[37] The defendants sold to the plaintiffs part of a quantity of white spirit being held for the defendants in the tank of a storage company. The defendants procured a delivery warrant from the storage company and made this over to the plaintiffs, who in turn indorsed it to their sub-purchaser. When the latter came to take delivery he found that the spirit had deteriorated in quality, and brought proceedings against the plaintiffs, who claimed over against the defendants.

The Court of Appeal held that even if the property in the spirit had not passed to the plaintiffs,[38] the defendants had done all they undertook to do, the plaintiffs could have withdrawn the spirit from storage at any time after delivery of the warrant to them and the proper inference was that the risk was to pass to them from that time.

Financing and security

Since each participant has different financial needs, tax and accounting requirements and credit ratings, it is not feasible for the licensee group as a whole to conclude a single financing arrangement. Instead, each participant arranges its own finance, whether from its own resources or from a bank against its name or against the project.

[36] Sale of Goods Act 1979, s.20(1). This, of course, assumes that the contract is governed by English law or by a foreign law which embodies a similar rule.

[37] [1923] 1 K.B. 78.

[38] And it is hard to see how it could have done, in view of s.16 of the Sale of Goods Act.

There are many different forms of secured[39] third-party finance, but I shall confine myself to three, namely the straight loan on the security of the project, the forward purchase and the production payment.

(1) *Loan on the security of the project*

Where the bank lends against the project it will normally expect to take security over the participant's licence interest, oil and gas entitlement, rights under supply contracts and proceeds of sale. There seems no reason why this should not be regarded as a normal security conferring real rights on the bank in the assets charged. The security would require to be registered under the Companies Act 1985, s.395, where the borrower company was registered in England or was an overseas company having an established place of business in England.[40]

Security in a licence interest and its fruits is inherently vulnerable. In the first place, the situation most likely to cause the debtor's default is a fall in the price of oil which makes future exploitation of the licensed area as unprofitable for the chargee as for the defaulting participant himself. Secondly, the operating agreement is likely to give the remaining participants a right to forfeit the defaulting party's interest where the default is protracted, and though the chargee may have negotiated the right to remedy the default this may involve expense disproportionate to the benefit gained. Thirdly, the circumstances of the default may well be such as to render the licence revocable by the Secretary of State.

(2) *Forward purchase*

Instead of lending on security, the financier can contract to purchase future oil acquired by the participant and to advance the price at interest, the participant's delivery obligation being discharged when the value of oil supplied to the financier (usually through direct delivery to a sub-purchaser) has reached the amount of the price and interest. Provided that the parties genuinely intend the financier to acquire title to the future oil supplies outright, and the participant has no right to "redeem" the oil, there is no reason why the courts should not treat the transaction as one of sale of goods, even though it is intended to fulfil a financing function. What matters is not the motive of the parties in choosing a particular legal

[39] The term "secured" is here used in a commercial rather than a legal sense, to embrace any form of financing arrangements intended as security.

[40] Companies Act 1985, s.409. The applicable heads of registration listed in s.396 would be, as regards the oil and gas and tangible proceeds, head (c) and, in the unlikely event of proceeds in the form of land, ships or aircraft, heads (d) and (h); as regards book debts arising from supply contracts, head (e); and as regards floating charges, regardless of the subject-matter, head (f).

form but the genuineness of the transaction, a point reiterated by the Court of Appeal in the recent decision in *Clough Mill Ltd.* v. *Martin*,[41] a case which I shall discuss in more detail in the final lecture of this series.[42] The fact that the financier may have reserved a right to require the participant to repurchase the oil at a later date in stated events would not by itself alter the legal character of the transaction as a sale.[43] The important point is that the participant has no *right* to re-acquire the oil by repayment, which is a crucial characteristic of a mortgage.

An analogy is readily to hand in receivables financing through a full-service factoring agreement. The factor agrees to buy a continuing stream of future trade debts and to advance part of the purchase price to the supplier-assignor, charging a discount for the period until maturity of the debt or such time as the factor himself assumes the risk of non-payment in respect of approved receivables. The supplier selling the debts is obliged to transfer receivables to at least the value of the price advanced, and is required to make good the deficiency in the event of any shortfall. The typical factoring agreement empowers the factor to require the supplier to repurchase receivables which are or become unapproved, but this does not affect the character of the transaction as an agreement for the sale and purchase of receivables.[44]

(3) *Production payment*

The production payment is a curious legal animal which has been highly developed in the United States, where it has long been established as a form of off-balance sheet financing of oil production. The production payment has been defined as:

> "a promise by the owner of a working interest under an oil and gas lease to deliver a fractional interest of the production of any or all of the minerals covered by the lease to the payee, or to pay him the monetary value thereof, until the payee has realized a certain sum from such deliveries or payments."[45]

Some, but not all, American jurisdictions recognize the transferability of oil and minerals *in situ*. As previously stated, English law

[41] [1984] 3 All E.R. 982.

[42] Below, pp. 98, 101.

[43] *Olds Discount Ltd.* v. *John Playfair Ltd.* [1938] 3 All E.R. 275; *Chow Yoong Hong* v. *Choong Fah Rubber Manufactory* [1962] A.C. 209.

[44] See cases cited above, n. 43, concerning block discounting of receivables.

[45] A. W. Walker Jr., *Oil Payments*, 20 Tex. L. Rev. 259, 262 (1942). For a detailed discussion of the production payment in relation to English law, see Lewis and Willoughby *loc. cit.* n. 20, above; Daintith and Willoughby; *op. cit.* n. 20, above, Chap. 4.

does not, so that all that could be conferred on the grantee of a production payment relating to an interest in oil *in situ* is a *profit à prendre*. Since ownership of all on-shore petroleum and exclusive rights over all offshore petroleum are vested in the Crown, the use of the American-style production payment is largely academic so far as this country is concerned.

However, there is nothing to prevent an equitable assignment of a fractional interest in extracted oil and its proceeds. Such an assignment would take effect in relation to any oil appropriated to the assignment by a contractually agreed act of ascertainment, and if so agreed this act of appropriation would also suffice to constitute the *novus actus* necessary to vest legal title in the transferee where the contract was not one of sale of goods.[46] The legal characterisation of the consideration for the assignment and of the assignment itself would depend on the nature of the agreement between the parties. If the assignment was by way of sale, the transaction would in essence be one of forward purchase previously described. If the finance was by way of loan and the assignment was on terms giving the assignor a right to redeem the transferred interest it would constitute a registrable mortgage. If, however, the assignment was an outright transfer, the assignor having no right to reacquire the transferred interest, it would not constitute a security interest even if the consideration for it was a loan. The assignor would simply be making an absolute disposition in or towards discharge of his indebtedness. Equally, the transaction would not be one of sale, since the sum paid by the financier was *ex hypothesi* advanced by way of loan, not paid as the price of oil under a contract of sale. Again, an analogy is to be found in receivables financing, as illustrated by the decision in *Siebe Gorman*,[47] where a company owing money to its bank made an outright assignment to the bank of a debt owed to the company. This was held not to constitute a mortgage or charge of a book debt, since the debt assigned, which was less than the amount owed to the bank, was intended to be given up permanently by the assignor, with no right of redemption. Nor, of course, was it a sale of a debt, since the original sum paid by the bank was paid not as the price of the debt but as a loan. So it is perfectly possible to transfer a chose in possession or a chose in action in or towards discharge of a debt without creating either a security interest or a sale. Moreover, the money laid out by the financier need not take the form of a loan. It could equally well be, for example, a payment as an equity participant, the transferred oil being in effect a return of capital invested plus any agreed interest.

[46] See above, p. 5.

[47] *Siebe Gorman & Co. Ltd.* v. *Barclays Bank Ltd.* [1979] 2 Lloyd's Rep. 142.

Gas and oil banking and substitution

Finally, a word about gas and oil banking and substitution. A licensee whose oil or gas is surplus to current requirements may "bank" it with another licensee who has a more immediate need, the latter undertaking to return an equivalent quantity of oil or gas to the depositor, less charges. Depositor and banker may also have concluded supply arrangements by which each of them is entitled to deliver to a purchaser gas coming from the other's field, or to deliver gas commingled from the two fields. The deposit of gas or oil under a banking scheme constitutes the loan of a fungible in exactly the same way as the deposit of money with a bank. Ownership passes to the banker on delivery and the banker incurs a personal obligation to return an equivalent quantity to the depositor, or deliver it to a third party at the depositor's direction. If the banker were to become insolvent before all the deposited oil or gas had been drawn (whether by the depositor itself or by delivery at its direction to a customer or other third party), the depositor would have no proprietary rights, merely a right to prove in the winding up.

III

Buying Through an Agent

The effect of an unauthorised sale by an agent, A, to a third party, T, of goods belonging to A's principal, P, has been widely discussed in legal literature. By contrast, there has been relatively little analysis of the problems of ownership that may arise where goods are sold *by T to A* and are then either claimed by P as having been bought for him or rejected by P as having been purchased by A without or in excess of authority. It is these problems on which I now propose to focus attention.

1. AGENCY ARRANGEMENTS

What is an agent?

Businessmen frequently appoint others to represent them in soliciting custom and in negotiating and concluding contracts. However, not all representatives are agents, and the commercial use of the term "agent" is broader than its legal signification.

In English law, an agent is one who agrees to represent another, the principal, for the purpose of creating or affecting a legal relationship between the principal and a third party.[1] A distributor who buys goods from a supplier and resells on his own account is thus not the supplier's agent in law, though in the commercial world he is not infrequently described as an agent. Where A at the request of P concludes a contract in his own name with T, A is liable to T on the contract, but under the doctrine of the undisclosed principal T has the option of suing P on discovering his existence as principal, and P can intervene to enforce the contract against T in place of A, except where A has been precluded by P or T from involving them in a contractual relationship with a third party. In the latter case, A is required to act as principal and is thus unable to commit P or T to each other, having merely an internal relationship with P governed by the terms of the agreement between them.[2] The concept of the undisclosed principal is peculiar to the common law. In civil law jurisdictions, if A contracts in his own name he does so as principal and no relationship of any kind is created between P and T. In short, the common law identifies the agent with the principal even where the latter is undisclosed, except where A is required by P or T to act on

[1] *Bowstead on Agency* (15th ed.), p. 1.
[2] See below.

his own behalf and not to involve any third party, whereas in the civil law A's use of his own name separates him from P, with the result that the agency agreement is a purely internal agreement between P and A which in principle has no effect on T.[3]

Agency distinguished from cases where A acts on his own account

There are many situations in which A is asked by P to assume an independent obligation to T, usually as a condition of T's willingness to deal with P. In these cases, although A acts on P's instructions in undertaking the commitment, he does so as principal. P is not even an undisclosed principal, for the intention is that A is to enter into a distinct contract with T separate from the main contract between P and T, typically on the basis that P will reimburse A and pay him a commission for his services. Among such contracts may be mentioned the following:

(1) *Guarantee of P's obligations*

P contracts to buy goods from T, who stipulates as a term of the sale contract that payment of the price, and possibly of P's other obligations, is to be guaranteed by a third party. At P's request, A acts as guarantor. His liability is a secondary one, being dependent on default by P, but it arises from a distinct contractual engagement. In furnishing the guarantee A acts on his own behalf. P's liability is on the principal contract, namely the sale agreement, not on the guarantee.

(2) *Assumption of parallel primary obligation*

P contracts to buy goods from T, who stipulates as a term of the sale contract that a third party (*e.g.* a bank or confirming house) is to assume primary responsibility for payment of the price. In some cases this responsibility is assumed by A as part and parcel of his agency activity in bringing about the sale contract, as where P's order for goods is routed through a confirming house, A, which places the order with the seller, T, on P's behalf and adds its own confirmation,[4] the effect being that T is to look to A in the first instance for payment of the price and can only have recourse to P if

[3] For an excellent analysis, see Clive M. Schmitthoff, *Agency in International Trade*. This principle of separation of the agency contract from the power of representation, though characteristic of agency in civil law jurisdictions, is not uniformly observed. Article 13(2) of the 1983 Geneva Convention on Agency in the International Sale of Goods represents an attempt to bridge the gap between the common law and civil law concepts. See below, p. 58.

[4] See, for example, *Sobell Industries Ltd.* v. *Cory Bros. & Co. Ltd.* [1955] 2 Lloyd's Rep. 82; and D. J. Hill, "Confirming house transactions in Commonwealth countries" 3 J. Mar. Law & Com. 307 (1972).

A defaults in payment. In other cases, the payment undertaking is given by one who has no involvement in the sale contract at all. The typical case is the irrevocable credit issued by a bank, A, at the request of its customer, P, the buyer of goods, by which A agrees to pay the seller, T, on presentation of designated shipping documents.

These cases differ from those described in (1) in that A is the first port of call for payment. It is only if A fails to pay or repudiates his payment obligation that T is entitled to look to P for payment.[5] A's undertaking is not given as agent for P but is a distinct, autonomous commitment. If A fails to pay, P is liable to T, not as the undisclosed principal on A's contract but as buyer under the contract of sale. The contractual method of payment (*i.e.* payment by A) having failed, the presumption is that T becomes entitled to look to P direct.[6]

(3) *Purchase as principal*

P asks A to purchase goods from T but not to involve P in any contractual relationship with T, even as undisclosed principal. This is the "commission agency" of the type familiar to civil layers but is not classified as an agency relationship in English law. Here, A purchases as principal and is the only person who can be sued for the price. P's existence may or may not be known to T but even where it is the effect of the contract or of usage is that A alone is to be liable to T. Property in the goods passes from A to P either by virtue of the terms of the mandate given by P or by way of resale.[7] Confirming houses sometimes undertake such commitments as principal and there are several Commonwealth decisions to support the proposition that under such an agreement the principal-agency relationship between P and A does not involve P in any commitment to T.[8] There is also powerful judicial support for such a concept in English law,[9] the most recent being a dictum of Roskill, L.J., in the famous

[5] *Stunzi Sons Ltd.* v. *House of Youth Pty. Ltd.* (1960) 60 S.R. (N.S.W.) 220; *Soproma SpA* v. *Marine & Animal By-Products Corp.* [1966] 1 Lloyd's Rep. 367, *per* McNair J. at p. 386; *W.J. Alan & Co. Ltd.* v. *El Nasr Export & Import Co.* [1972] 2 Q.B. 189.

[6] *E.D. & F. Man Ltd.* v. *Nigerian Sweets & Confectionery Co. Ltd.* [1977] 2 Lloyd's Rep. 50; *Maran Road Saw Mill* v. *Austin Taylor & Co. Ltd.* [1975] 1 Lloyd's Rep. 156; *W.J. Alan & Co. Ltd.* v. *El Nasr. Export & Import Co.*, *supra*; and see E. P. Ellinger (1977) 40 M.L.R. 91.

[7] See below, p. 50.

[8] See, for example, *Bolus & Co. Ltd.* v. *Inglis* [1924] N.Z.L.R. 175; *Witt & Scott Ltd.* v. *Blumenreich* [1949] N.Z.L.R. 806. See also *Rusholme & Bolton & Roberts Hadfield Ltd.* v. *S.G. Read & Co. Ltd.* [1955] 1 W.L.R. 146, where A was held liable, though it is not clear whether the court considered there was no liability on P.

[9] *Ireland* v. *Livingstone* (1872) L.R 5 H.L. 395, *per* Lord Blackburn at p. 408; *Cassaboglou* v. *Gibb* (1883) 11 Q.B.D. 797; *Aluminium Industrie Vaassen B.V.* v. *Romalpa Aluminium Ltd.* [1976] 1 Lloyd's Rep. 443, at p. 456. *cf. E. Bailey & Co. Ltd.* v. *Balholm Securities Ltd.* [1973] 2 Lloyd's Rep. 404 at p. 408. See also F. M. B. Reynolds, "Agency: Theory and Practice" (1978) 94 L.Q.R. 224 at p. 233.

Romalpa case, where the court was considering the converse position of A buying goods from P under reservation of title and selling them to T as principal but pursuant to a mandate from P.

> "I see no difficulty in the contractual concept that, as between the appellants and their sub-purchasers, the appellants sold as principals, but that, as between themselves and the respondents, those goods which they were selling as principals within their implied authority from the respondents were the respondents' goods which they were selling as agents for the respondents to whom they remained fully accountable."[10]

The three types of agency relationship

If we exclude the case where A's role is purely that of surety, we are left with at least three different agency models. The first is a purchase by A expressly as agent, with or without disclosing P's identity (figure 1). In this situation T knows that he is dealing through an agent, though he does not necessarily know the name of the buyer. The second is a purchase by A as apparent principal but in reality as agent for P (figure 2). Here T is unaware that there is any principal standing behind A. Nevertheless, T may find himself dealing with P if the latter chooses to intervene and conversely may elect to hold P liable instead of A. The third model is a purchase by A on P's instructions but as the true principal, buying on his own account but with a duty to transfer the goods to P pursuant to the agreement between them[11] (figure 3).

AGENCY MODELS

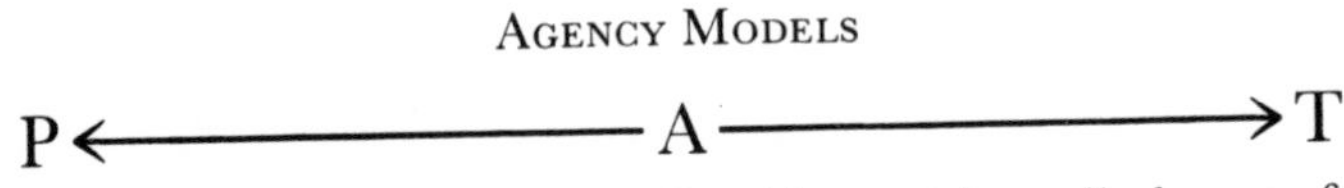

Fig. 1 Sale through A as agent to P, with or without disclosure of P's identity.

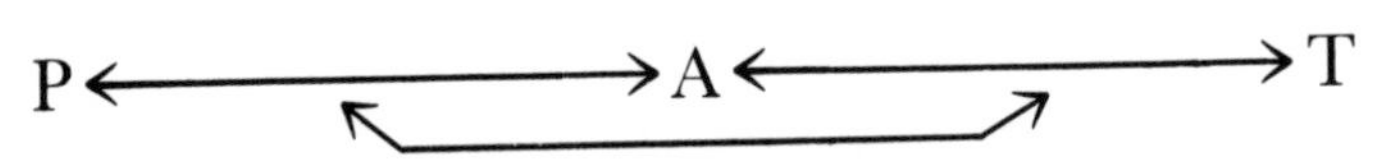

Fig. 2 Sale to A as apparent principal but in reality as agent for an undisclosed principal, P. The contract is between T and A but T may elect to hold P liable and P may intervene to enforce the contract.

[10] *Aluminium Industrie Vaassen B.V.* v. *Romalpa Aluminium Ltd.* [1976] 1 Lloyd's Rep. 443 at p. 456.

[11] This model falls outside the conventional definition of agency. See above, pp. 41 and 43.

Fig. 3 Sale to A as true principal, with no relationship between T and P. A transfers goods to P under their agreement, as agent or by way of resale.

2. THE TRANSFER OF TITLE BY T: GENERAL CONSIDERATIONS

Alternative effects of a transfer by T

Where A, on the instructions of P, concludes a contract to purchase goods from T as the result of which T divests himself of title, there are at least five alternative proprietary effects:

(1) legal and beneficial ownership pass directly to P without going through A;
(2) legal and beneficial ownership pass to P through A;
(3) legal title passes to A but equitable ownership vests in P, *i.e.* A holds on trust for P;
(4) legal and beneficial ownership pass to A, who holds possession for P pursuant to a prior or contemporaneous attornment;
(5) P acquires no rights *in rem* upon the sale, merely a contractual right to require A to transfer ownership and possession to him.

So long as A remains solvent and performs his obligations to P, it makes little difference which of the above alternatives applies. However, if A becomes bankrupt or wrongfully disposes of the goods before P has acquired any rights *in rem*, P is likely to find himself in the position of an unsecured creditor, with potentially heavy losses. I shall now consider the impact of these adverse events in each of the five alternative situations set out above, and will then go on to discuss the ways in which different kinds of proprietary right may vest in P so as to protect his position.

Case 1—Legal and beneficial ownership pass directly to P

This, of course, is the best case for P. If A becomes insolvent before P has acquired possession, P is entitled to enforce his title against A's trustee and creditors subject to any lien or right of stoppage in transit which A may have as a deemed unpaid seller to secure charges or reimbursement of expenses due from P to A.[12]

[12] The rights of the unpaid seller, including his lien and right of stoppage, are set out in the Sale of Goods Act 1979, ss.39–46. By s.38(2) "seller" includes "any person who is in the position of a seller, as, for instance, an agent of the seller to whom the bill of lading has been indorsed, or a consignor or agent who has himself paid (or is directly responsible for) the price."

If A, though not becoming insolvent, wrongfully disposes of the goods to a third party, X, then P is entitled to recover the goods from X under the principle *nemo dat quod non habet*[13] except in those cases where X acquires an overriding title. P's title may be overridden where A sells the goods to X in market overt[14] or while acting in the ordinary course of business as a mercantile agent,[15] though in the latter case P will lose title only if it can be shown that he consented to A's taking or retaining possession in his capacity as mercantile agent, *e.g.* to sell it, offer it for sale or display it in his showroom.[16]

Case 2—Legal and beneficial ownership pass to P through A

The case here postulated is that by virtue of a prior agreement between A and P title passes from A to P the moment it is acquired by A. The results are the same as in Case 1, for there is no *scintilla temporis* between A's acquisition of ownership and its transfer to P and thus no scope for A's trustee or a third party to assert an overriding interest otherwise than by virtue of some exception to the *nemo dat* rule as described above.

Case 3—A acquires legal title but holds on trust for B

The position is very nearly, but not quite, the same as in Cases 1 and 2. Subject to the same exceptions as described above, P's equitable ownership is as effective against A's trustee in bankruptcy as full legal title, since property held on trust by the bankrupt does not form part of his estate.[17] If A, in breach of his duty to make over the goods to P, disposes of them to X, P as the person entitled to possession can maintain an action for conversion against A and also against X except where the latter acquires an overriding title. Two statutory exceptions to the *nemo dat* rule have already been noted. However, the fact that in Case 3 P's ownership is purely equitable will also enable X to defeat P's claim at common law if X acquires the legal title as a bona fide purchaser for value without notice of P's rights. This is simply an application of the general rule of common law giving priority to a legal purchaser for value without notice over the holder of a prior equitable interest.[18] In such a case, P's rights will shift from the goods themselves to their proceeds in the hands of A.

[13] Sale of Goods Act 1979, s.21.
[14] *Ibid.* s.22.
[15] Factors Act 1889, s.2.
[16] *Astley Industrial Trust Ltd.* v. *Miller* [1968] 2 All E.R. 36.
[17] Insolvency Act 1986, s.283(3)(a).
[18] See *Snell's Principles of Equity* (28th ed.), pp. 48 *et seq.*

Case 4—legal and beneficial ownership in A, who attorns to P

Even where both legal and beneficial ownership have been transferred to A, this does not necessarily mean that P has no real right in the goods at the time A acquires them, for A may have previously agreed to hold the goods for P or may do so at the moment he receives them. In either case, A's attornment to P becomes effective at the moment when A receives the goods, so that P has constructive possession.[19] This is a real right enforceable against A's trustee in bankruptcy.[20] The quantum of a possessory interest is measured by the agreement under which possession is held.[21] P is thus entitled to take physical possession of the goods from A's trustee and to hold it indefinitely, for *ex hypothesi* his agreement with A entitles him to call for a transfer of title which would result in his becoming the absolute owner with a perpetual right of possession, and A's trustee succeeds to A's title subject to P's possessory interest.[22] The trustee's refusal to surrender the goods would expose him to an action for conversion by P for wrongful interference with his possession.

Where A wrongfully disposes of the goods to X, P's position is very weak. His possessory title is destroyed, for X's intention is to possess not for P but for himself, and whilst P could maintain an action for conversion if he could show that he had the best right to possession and that right was interfered with by X, X's acquisition of ownership (whether legal or equitable) overrides P's personal right to possession unless X takes as a donee or with notice of P's rights.[23]

Case 5—P acquires no rights in rem

Where legal and beneficial ownership pass to A who holds possession *animo domino* or for a limited interest of his own (*e.g.* by way of lien to secure unpaid charges due from P), P has no real right in the goods, merely a contractual right to require A to transfer them to him. Such a contractual right is not enforceable against A's trustee in bankruptcy, and if the trustee refuses to carry out the contract P is left with a right to prove in the bankruptcy. Similarly, A's contractual right to the goods is not enforceable against X unless he takes as a volunteer or with notice of the right.

It will be apparent, therefore, that P's best protection against the

[19] *Hall* v. *Griffin* (1833) 10 Bing. 246, *per* Tindal C.J. at p. 248; and see generally above, p. 9.
[20] See above, pp. 1, 3, 7.
[21] See above, p. 7; and R. M. Goode, *Commercial Law*, pp. 53–54, 61.
[22] See above, pp. 7, 14.
[23] In the latter case, X is exposed to an alternative claim in tort for interference with the contract between A and P.

consequences of A's bankruptcy or wrongful disposition of the goods to X is full legal ownership, but that failing this some lesser real right—equitable ownership or even a mere possessory interest—may serve the purpose. Accordingly we must now turn to consider how these various forms of real right are acquired by P consequent upon the sale by T.

3. THE ACQUISITION OF FULL LEGAL TITLE BY P

Two fundamental principles

The transfer of legal title from one person to another is governed by two fundamental legal principles:

(1) *Legal title passes to the person intended by the transferor*

The transfer of any asset depends on the will of the transferor, express or implied. If T sells goods to A intending that title shall vest in A, the law will give effect to this intention. A may have agreed with P to hold the goods on trust for him, or T may stipulate that A is to hold the goods on trust for P, but that does not affect the legal title. Indeed, the whole concept of equitable ownership presupposes that legal title is in one person—in our example, A, the person designated by T as the transferee—and beneficial ownership in another.[24]

(2) *Legal title to goods passes under a contract only when the goods are identified and the transferor intends title to pass*

This second rule is clearly expressed by sections 16 and 17 of the Sale of Goods Act 1979 in relation to contracts of sale. The time when title passes from seller to buyer depends primarily on the intention of the parties,[25] and rules as to their presumed intention are laid down in section 18 of the Act. The intention of the parties, however clearly expressed, cannot be effectuated unless the goods are identified, either at the time of the contract or by a subsequent act of appropriation.[26] Section 16 of the Act is the overriding provision; if we cannot tell which are the goods to which the contract of sale relates, the intention of the parties to transfer title counts for nothing.

[24] This is why arguments sometimes advanced that the equitable right to trace should be extended to cases where the plaintiff has both legal and beneficial ownership are misconceived, for where the same person is entitled both legally and beneficially he does not have a legal title and a separate equitable interest, he is simply the full legal owner. It was for this reason that Slade J. rightly held in *Re Bond Worth Ltd.* [1980] Ch. 228 that upon the sale of goods it was not possible for the seller to "reserve" equitable ownership, and a purported reservation of equitable ownership was to be construed as a grant back by the buyer.

[25] Sale of Goods Act 1979, s.17.

[26] *Ibid.* s.16. See above, pp. 17 *et seq.*

Transfer of title direct from T to P

P will acquire legal title to identified goods direct from T if and when so intended by T. What if T knows that A is acting as agent and intends to pass title to A's principal but does not know that principal's identity? Since P is in fact the principal, does this suffice to give effect to T's intention and transfer legal title to P? Probably it does. It is certainly not necessary for T to know P, or for the contract of sale to identify P, by name. It suffices that P is identifiable from the terms of the contract concluded through A's agency. If T stipulates that title is to pass to whoever is A's principal and it can be established that A was indeed acting for P in the purchase and not on his own account or as agent for some other principal,[27] there seems no reason why legal title should not pass directly to P even though his identity is unknown to T.

Transfer of title to P through A

This is a much more likely situation. A acquires ownership from T, as intended by T, and simultaneously this passes from A to P. In order for this to occur, three conditions must be fulfilled by the time A himself acquires ownership from T:

(1) the goods must be identified;
(2) A must appropriate them to his mandate from P, that is, perform some act evincing his intention to earmark the goods unconditionally to that mandate;
(3) A must intend title to pass to P.

In short, whether A passes title as a sub-seller or purely as an agent,[28] the same conditions must be satisfied as on a sale by A to P. Where A's act of appropriation, coupled with an intention to transfer title to P, precedes the sale from T to A, the effect of that sale is to feed title through to P simultaneously, so that there is no interval of time between A's acquisition of title and his loss of it in favour of P. Where either A's act of appropriation is not made or his intention to transfer title to P is not formed until after A has acquired title, there will be an interval in which P's position is exposed to the possibility of A's bankruptcy or unauthorised disposition to X.

What constitutes a sufficient act of appropriation by A is to be determined in accordance with the principles discussed earlier.[29] In general, the act must either be one which is specifically assented to by P at or after the time it has been done or must be an act which puts the goods outside A's control, as where, having received a bill of

[27] See below, pp. 51 *et seq.*
[28] See below.
[29] See above, pp. 17 *et seq.*

lading from T consigning the goods to him, A indorses the bill of lading in favour of P.

The capacity in which A acts when passing title on to P depends on the agreement between them. The general relationship will be that of principal and agent by which A is given a mandate to purchase goods from T on his own account and then transfer them to P, but that transfer may be made either under a contract for resale to P or simply pursuant to an agency duty.[30] In both cases, A has a lien and right of stoppage to secure the payment due to him, whether for the price where he acts as seller or for his commission and expenses where he acts as agent, for in the latter case he is equated with an unpaid seller.[31] In other respects the distinction between A's two alternative capacities may be very material to P's rights. Where A acts as seller, he has a right to be paid the purchase price as such and conversely owes a strict duty to supply the goods in accordance with the contract of sale; where he is to transfer the goods as agent, his money entitlement is usually in the form of a commission for his services and his duty is limited to the exercise of reasonable care and skill.[31] If A fails to deliver the goods to P pursuant to a contract of sale, P is entitled to damages for loss of a bargain, represented by the difference between the market price at the due date of delivery and the contract price[32]; where his delivery obligation is as agent, P's claim for breach of that duty is limited to the loss he actually suffers.[33] Finally—and most significantly for our purposes—where A is to transfer the goods to B by way of resale, P acquires no equitable interest in the goods until transfer of the legal title to him,[34] and meanwhile has a mere contract right which will not avail against A's trustee or a bona fide purchaser for value from A without notice, whereas if the duty to transfer is an agency duty then A holds the goods as trustee for P until their appropriation,[35] and P can assert his equitable ownership against A's trustee and any third party other than a bona fide purchaser of *the legal title* for value and without notice.

Lastly, though P's acquisition of legal title depends on identification of the goods to A's mandate, once legal title has become vested in P then on the *subsequent* wrongful commingling of the goods with those of A or X, P is entitled to assert either a proprietary interest in the new product (sole or in common with others, depending on

[30] *Ireland* v. *Livingstone* (1872) L.R 5 H.L. 395, as explained in *Cassaboglou* v. *Gibb* (1883) 11 Q.B.D. 797.
[31] *Ibid.*; Sale of Goods Act, s.38(2).
[32] Sale of Goods Act, s.51(3).
[33] *Cassaboglou* v. *Gibb*, above.
[34] See above, p. 6.
[35] Upon appropriation the legal title passes.

the circumstances) or title to the whole product where it results from A's intentional wrongdoing in mixing his goods with those of P.[36]

4. THE ACQUISITION OF EQUITABLE OWNERSHIP BY P

When equitable ownership will vest in P

P acquires equitable ownership of goods acquired by A from T (*i.e.* A will hold them as P's trustee) where T transfers legal title to A and:

(1) T imposes the trust on A when selling to him;
(2) A buys the goods for the purpose of transferring them to P as agent or by way of sub-sale but has not appropriated them to P[37];
(3) A declares himself a trustee for P;
(4) an equivocal transaction concluded by A is resolved in P's favour in accordance with the principles discussed in Section 6, below.

Where P has acquired equitable ownership the rules as to his rights where the goods later become commingled with other goods are the same as where P is the full legal owner.

5. ATTORNMENT IN FAVOUR OF P

When attornment occurs

As we have seen, even where neither legal nor equitable title passes to P he may acquire constructive possession as the result of A's attornment. This may occur either where A is in physical possession and attorns to P or where A is himself in constructive possession (*e.g.* through attornment to him by T or by a carrier or warehouse) and holds constructive possession on behalf of P.[38] In such a case, the carrier or warehouse itself probably shares possession only with A, not with P, but P as the principal for whom A holds constructive possession has the right to intervene and substitute himself as the bailor.[39]

6. EQUIVOCAL TRANSACTIONS

So far, we have assumed that A, when buying the goods from T, acts on a mandate from P to buy either for P directly or on his own account but with a duty to transfer the goods on to P. However,

[36] See below, p. 90.
[37] See above, pp. 17, 49.
[38] See below.
[39] See above, p. 11.

there may be cases where it is not clear whether A acted for P or on his own behalf or for another principal, P2. Where then does P stand? For simplicity I shall confine myself to the case where A's mandate is to buy goods not on his own account but for P as disclosed or undisclosed principal and A in fact makes a purchase in his own name. Three typical situations will be examined.

(1) *A is authorised by P to buy and is put in funds by P but claims to have bought on his own account*

Where A expresses himself as buying on behalf of P there is little difficulty. The problem arises where A, having obtained funds from P, contracts to buy in his own name and then becomes insolvent after spending the money given to him. P claims the goods; A's trustee replies that there is nothing to show that A was not making a purchase on his own account, as he was entitled to do. Who wins?

Let us start with the easy cases. If A undertakes to buy identified goods for P and then purports to buy them on his own account, he will be considered a trustee for P. It does not matter whether A used P's money or his own; he has a fiduciary duty to transfer the goods to P and will be considered a constructive trustee for P.[40] Next, if A receives funds from P which are to be specifically applied to the purchase of goods from T and A uses the funds for that purpose, he holds the goods on trust for P.[41] In this case, it is not necessary that the goods shall have been identified to A's mandate. It suffices that they are bought with P's funds. This is easily established where A placed the funds in a separate account and then drawn on that account when paying the price to T. The *locus classicus* is the colourful case of *Taylor* v. *Plumer*.[42] The defendant gave his stockbroker a banker's draft with instructions to apply the proceeds of the draft in the purchase of Exchequer bills and lodge these with the defendant's bankers. The stockbroker used part of the proceeds for this purpose but fraudulently misapplied the balance in the purchase of securities and bullion for his own benefit. He then became insolvent and sought to evade his creditors by fleeing to America but was caught at Falmouth and then surrendered the securities and bullion to the defendants. His assignees in bankruptcy then sued the defendants in trover for delivery up of the securities and bullion. It was held that both at law and in equity these belonged to the defendants, having been acquired with their property.[43]

40 *Lees* v. *Nuttall* (1829) 1 Russ. & M. 53; *Chattock* v. *Muller* (1878) 8 Ch.D. 177; *Pallant* v. *Morgan* [1953] Ch. 43.

41 *Taylor* v. *Plumer* (1815) 3 M. & S. 562; *Harris* v. *Truman & Co.* (1882) 9 Q.B.D. 264; *James* v. *Smith* [1891] 1 Ch.D. 84; *Regier* v. *Campbell-Stuart* [1939] Ch. 766.

42 Above.

43 For a discussion of the case, see R. M. Goode, "The Right to Trace and its Impact in Commercial Transactions" (1976) 92 L.Q.R. 360 at pp. 367 *et seq.*

But what if A, though receiving moneys from P on terms that they are to be kept separate and applied specifically for the purchase of generic goods[44] from T, in fact commingles them with his own moneys and then purchases the goods from the mixed fund and asserts that he bought them for his own account? This case is more difficult. Had the use of trust funds to purchase the goods been unlawful, P would have a choice. He could invoke the presumption against A's committing a breach of trust and thus claim that A's own moneys should as far as possible be treated as applied to the purchase, leaving P's fund intact.[45] Alternatively, he could claim a lien on the mixed fund to the extent of his payment, if part of the fund was still in existence, together with a concurrent lien on the goods or, at his option, a share in the goods proportionate to the amount of the trust moneys employed in their purchase.[46] What complicates the situation in our example is that the only impropriety A has committed is in mixing P's money with his own. A is perfectly within his rights in using P's money to buy goods *for P*, for that is what he was instructed to do, so that the presumption against committing a breach of trust does not come into play. Equally, so long as he does not use P's money he is entitled to buy goods of the same description for his own account. If A's portion of the mixed fund was sufficient in amount to cover the price of the purchase from T without resorting to P's moneys, A's conduct, though capable of being construed as an attempt to use P's money to buy goods for A's own benefit, is also referable to his entirely legitimate decision to use his own money to buy the goods for his own account; and since P's instructions referred only to the acquisition of generic goods, P is not in a position to say that the goods in fact purchased by A are attributable to the mandate from P. If the rest of the fund has been dissipated since the purchase, P will argue in favour of the latter interpretation of A's conduct whilst A's trustee will contend for the former. The answer would seem to be that, since A has wrongfully destroyed the identity of P's fund by mixing it with his own moneys, the law does not require P to invoke any particular rule of appropriation in order to determine whose money was used to purchase the goods but entitles him to assert a charge on the mixed fund to secure his own money and subsequently, when the whole or part of the fund has been applied to the purchase of the goods, a charge on the goods and on any residue of the fund to secure that money. In other words,

[44] If A's mandate is to buy specific goods, which are then purchased by A, it is irrelevant whether they were bought with P's money or with A's. See text to n. 40, *supra*.

[45] *Re Hallett's Estate* (1880) 13 Ch.D. 696; *Re Oatway* [1903] 2 Ch. 356; *Re Tilley's Will Trusts* [1967] Ch. 1179; and see Goode, *loc. cit.* n. 43, *supra*, at pp. 537–538 and Keeton and Sheridan, *Equity* (3rd ed.), p. 506.

[46] *Ibid.*

A cannot rely on his own wrongful act of commingling to impose on P the burden of identifying which part of the mixed fund was used for the purchase of the goods; and since A's trustee cannot be in any better position than A himself, P is entitled to a charge on the goods and on any residue in A's account to secure recoupment of the money deposited with A.[47] Alternatively, P can claim a share of the goods proportionate to the amount of the trust moneys employed in its purchase, calculated on the assumption that A used his own moneys first,[48] together with a charge on any unexpended balance of the mixed fund to secure that part of his original fund which was not employed in the purchase of the goods.

The position is otherwise, of course, if A dissipates P's funds and uses his own money to buy the goods for his own account. In such a case, P has no claim to the goods and is merely an unsecured creditor.

Finally, let us suppose that the money given by P to A was not impressed with a trust and was merely lent to or deposited with A on terms that he could treat it as his own and commingle it with his other moneys, being merely a debtor to P with a right to be reimbursed for any expenses incurred in buying the goods from T on P's behalf. If A then buys goods of the same description from T on his own account, P has no proprietary claim either to the money deposited with A or to the goods, for *ex hypothesi* the money used by A to purchase the goods was his own, the purchase is not unequivocally referable to A's mandate from P and in buying for his own account A is not committing any breach of duty to P.

(2) *A is authorised by different principals to buy and is put in funds by them but fails to identify the principal for whom he buys*

Let us suppose that A receives instructions to buy goods of the same description for two different principals P1 and P2, purchases from T as agent but fails to identify his principal at the time of the purchase and becomes bankrupt without having appropriated the goods either to P1 or to P2. Who is entitled to the goods? Such a problem is by no means academic. It can arise in practice in a variety of contexts, including agency equipment leasing, where A has agreements with two or more leasing companies each of which authorises him, within defined limits, to purchase equipment as apparent principal but in reality as agent for the leasing company concerned, which will then let this to A on lease.

The governing principles are the same as those described in the first case. If it can be shown that the goods were bought with P1's

[47] *Re Hallett's Estate, supra*; *Sinclair* v. *Brougham* [1914] A.C. 398, *per* Lord Parker of Waddington at p. 442.

[48] See *Re Tilley's Will Trusts* [1967] Ch. 1179; Keeton and Sheridan, *op. cit.*, p. 506.

money, or if A's mandate from P1 related exclusively to the specific goods bought and A's mandate from P2 did not, the goods belong in equity to P1 except so far as, in the latter case, the purchase of the specific goods was made with P2's money. If the goods were bought with a mixed fund comprising partly money belonging to P1 and partly money belonging to P2, the two principals become tenants in common in equity in the proportions of their respective contributions to the price. If the mixed fund also comprised money belonging to A, P1 and P2 have the option of claiming a charge on the goods, and on any unexpended balance of the mixed fund, to secure recoupment of their outlay or a proportionate interest in the goods and a charge on the unexpended balance of the mixed fund to secure recoupment of that part of their funds not applied in the purchase of the goods.

Where, however, both P1 and P2 instruct A to make a purchase of the same identified goods from T, and A does so with his own money without identifying his principal or making an appropriation as between them, then it would seem that on A's bankruptcy the goods form part of his estate, for there is no way of telling who his principal is. P1 and P2 cannot, it is thought, claim an equitable tenancy in common for in making his purchase A neither used their moneys nor had authority to buy for them in common. Since in such a case the onus is on the claimant to prove his title, and neither of the parties can do so, the goods can be claimed by A's trustee.

Where A's mandate from the two principals relates to generic goods and he buys in his own name with his own money and makes no appropriation, before becoming bankrupt, the goods form part of his estate, for there is nothing to connect them with either of the two mandates given to A.

(3) *A is authorised by different principals to buy, is put in funds and after purchase purports to appropriate to both of them*

This is the converse of case (2). In accordance with instructions received separately from P1 and P2 A buys goods, either as apparent principal or as agent for an unidentified principal, and then purports to appropriate the goods to both mandates, after which he becomes insolvent. If P1's mandate related exclusively to the specific goods bought and P2's mandate did not, then except so far as P2's money was used for the purchase P1 acquires sole ownership, for his rights do not depend on any act of appropriation by A. To the extent to which the funds of P1 or P2 were employed in the purchase of the goods, each has a share in the goods. If the same specific goods were called for both by P1 and by P2 and were bought by A with his own money before becoming bankrupt, the goods pass to his trustee and cannot be claimed by either of his principals, for the reason given earlier. *A fortiori*, if both mandates related to generic goods and the goods were bought with A's own money, then on his bankruptcy without making any appropriation the goods form part of his estate.

7. PURCHASE WITHOUT OR IN EXCESS OF AUTHORITY

Apparent authority equated with actual authority

So far, we have assumed that A has authority to buy goods for P and that when doing so he acts within the limits of that authority. However, it sometimes happens that A purports to act for P when he has no authority to do so or alternatively exceeds the limits of the authority given to him. In such a case, the rule is that as between P and T, A's apparent, or ostensible, authority is equated with actual authority. But "apparent authority" does not mean merely the appearance of authority; the phrase is legal shorthand to denote an appearance of authority to which P has in some way lent himself, through conduct by which P holds A out as authorised to that which he in fact did. I shall not dwell further on this particular topic, which is fully analysed in the textbooks.[49] What I propose to consider now is the situation that arises where A buys goods for P without either actual or apparent authority to do so. In making his purchase, A may declare himself to be acting for P, or he may contract expressly as agent but without identifying his principal or he may contract as apparent principal. Each of these possibilities will now be considered in turn.

Purchase by A expressed to be as agent for P

A buys from T and does so expressly as P's agent. Four alternative cases now fall to be examined.

(1) *P exists and ratifies A's action*

Thereupon, a contract of sale is created between T and P which takes effect as from the date of A's agreement with T, as if A had been authorised from the outset.[50]

(2) *P exists but fails or refuses to ratify*

In this case, there is generally no effective contract of sale at all.[51] T's remedy is to sue A for damages for breach of warranty of authority.[52] The nature or terms of the contract or the surrounding circumstances however, may show that the intention of A and T,

[49] *Bowstead on Agency* (15th ed.), art. 76; G. H. L. Fridman, *Law of Agency* (5th ed.), pp. 105 *et seq.*
[50] *Bolton Partners* v. *Lambert* (1884) 41 Ch.D. 295.
[51] *Lewis* v. *Nicholson* (1852) 18 Q.B. 503.
[52] *Collen* v. *Wright* (1857) 8 E. & B. 647.

viewed objectively, was that A should assume liability on the contract as well as or in place of P, in which event the law will give effect to that intention.[53]

(3) *P does not exist at the time of the alleged contract but comes into existence subsequently and purports to ratify*

P's purported ratification of a contract made before P came into existence is ineffective.[54] At common law, A might also have been able to escape liability,[55] but the effect of section 36(4) of the Companies Act 1985[56] is to make A personally liable, subject to any contrary agreement between A and T.[57] The result is that a contract of sale comes into existence between T and A and any title transferred under that contract vests in A.

(4) *P does not exist at the time of the alleged contract and either never comes into existence or does so but does not ratify*

The position is the same as in Case (3).

Purchase by A expressed to be as agent but without identifying P

Where A, with P's authority, buys expressly as agent for an unidentified principal, the general rule is that T's contract is with P and not with A.[58] However, A may become liable on the contract if he refuses to disclose P's identity[59] or if the intention of T and A, viewed objectively, is that A is to assume personal liability.[60]

Where A acts without authority, it would seem that P can ratify the contract, at least if it can be established that P, though not named, can be identified from the terms of the contract as A's principal in relation to the transaction.[61]

[53] *Bridges & Salmon Ltd.* v. *The Swan, The Swan* [1968] 1 Lloyd's Rep. 5; F. M. B. Reynolds, (1967) 85 L.Q.R. 92.

[54] *Kelner* v. *Baxter* (1866) L.R. 2 C.P. 174; *Newborne* v. *Sensolid (Great Britain) Ltd.* [1954] 1 Q.B. 45.

[55] *Newborne* v. *Sensolid (Great Britain) Ltd.*, above.

[56] Re-enacting s.9(2) of the European Communities Act 1972.

[57] As to which see *Phonogram Ltd.* v. *Lane* [1982] Q.B. 938.

[58] At one time this rule was thought not to apply in the case of a foreign principal, but the present position is that this fact does not exclude the rule but is merely a factor to be taken into account in determining whether it is intended that the agent shall be personally liable (*Teheran-Europe Co. Ltd.* v. *S.T. Belton (Tractors) Ltd.* [1968] 2 Q.B. 545).

[59] *Herson* v. *Bernett* [1955] 1 Q.B. 98.

[60] See F. M. B. Reynolds (1978) 94 L.Q.R 224 at p. 230.

[61] See *Bowstead on Agency* (15th ed.), pp. 61–63.

Purchase by A as apparent principal

Where A buys from T as apparent principal but in reality on behalf of and by authority of P, the contract of sale is between T and A, but P may elect to intervene and enforce the contract for his own benefit,[62] whilst T, if he discovers P's existence as principal, may elect to sue him instead of A.[63]

Where A contracts in his own name without P's authority, only A can sue and be sued on the contract, and title passes to him. P cannot ratify the contract in such a case, for ratification is permitted only by the person on whose behalf A expresses himself as acting and is thus not available where A contracts as principal.[64]

8. AGENCY IN INTERNATIONAL SALES

In conclusion, I would draw your attention to the 1983 Geneva Convention on Agency in the International Sale of Goods, which regulates the relations between the third party and the principal and the agent in relations to contracts for the international sale of goods. This Convention, which does not govern the relations of principal and agent *inter se*, adopts rules differing in various respects from those of the common law, though in large measure the Convention rules would be familiar to a common lawyer. By Article 2(1), the Convention, which has not yet been ratified by the United Kingdom, applies only where the principal and the third party have their places of business in different States and:

(a) the agent has his place of business in a Contracting State; or
(b) the rules of private international law lead to the application of the law of a Contracting State.

By Article 2(2), where, at the time of contracting, the third party neither knew nor ought to have known that the agent was acting as an agent, the Convention applies only if the agent and the third party had their places in different States and the requirements of Article 2(1) are satisfied.

[62] *Ibid.* art. 82 and Comment.
[63] *Ibid.*
[64] *Keighley Maxsted & Co.* v. *Durant* [1901] A.C. 240.

IV

Dealings in Warehoused Goods and Goods in Transit

1. THE NATURE AND EFFECT OF A DOCUMENT OF TITLE

The function of documents of title

Many people—even lawyers—have only the haziest notion of the function of a document of title to goods. They know that on the sale of land the vendor is invariably required to hand over to the purchaser the documents of title: in the case of unregistered land, the title deeds; in the case of registered land, the land certificate. In general, there is no great difficulty in deducing title to land, because each parcel of land is unique, permanent and static and because the law severely restricts what the purchaser can call for. As regards unregistered land, the most he can demand is the title deeds going back to a root of title not less than 15 years old which constitutes in other respects a good root of title.[1] Where title is registered, the investigation of prior ownership will have been carried out for the purpose of first registration, and the land certificate is all that is needed for this purpose.

Chattels are entirely different. Their mobility, lack of permanence and relative fungibility make it pointless to bring into existence any permanent record of a chain of ownership, so that in most cases it would be difficult, if not impossible, to trace the history of a chattel's ownership right back to the ownership of the various raw materials from which it was made. It follows that whilst the *raison d'être* of a document of title to land is to give its owner a written assurance of his title which he will hold so long as his ownership continues, the document of title to goods fulfils a quite different function. Such a document comes into existence to facilitate dealings in goods which are not in the physical possession of the transferor but are held for him by a bailee, typically for the purpose of storage in a warehouse or transportation by sea. In essence a document of title to goods embodies the undertaking of the bailee to hold the goods for whoever is the current holder of the document and to deliver it up to such person in exchange for the document. Hence the document of title is a vehicle for transferring *control* (i.e. constructive possession), not ownership; indeed, it would be more accurate to describe it as a

[1] Law of Property Act 1969, s.23.

"control document" rather than a document of title. It is true that under the express or implied terms of the contract of sale or other agreement between transferor and transferee the property in the goods may be made to pass on delivery of the document of title but this results from the agreement, not from the status of the document of title as such. The delivery of the document is simply a convenient mechanism for implementing the contract between the parties in relation to the transfer of ownership. It is not, however, a necessary mechanism; the parties can, and frequently do, agree to divorce the transfer of property in the goods from the delivery of the document, as by stipulating that ownership is to pass only upon payment.

Thus a document of title can be said to fulfil two functions in relation to the transfer of rights *in rem*. The first and primary function is to enable control of warehoused goods or goods in transit to be transferred by delivery of the document with any necessary indorsement. The bailee issues what is in effect a negotiable receipt by which he undertakes to hold the goods for whoever is in for the time being in possession of the receipt and to release the goods to the person producing the receipt, whether he be the original bailor or a transferee of the document. Like a negotiable instrument, the receipt is transferred by delivery with any necessary indorsement.[2] Possession of the receipt confers on the holder constructive possession of the goods to which it relates, so long as these are identified and not an unascertained part of a bulk. Once the receipt has been handed back to the bailee in exchange for the goods or the bailee loses possession in some other manner (*e.g.* by releasing the goods without production of the receipt, against an indemnity), the function of the receipt as a document of title is exhausted and it ceases to have legal effect as an instrument of control of the goods. The second and subsidiary function of the document of title is to provide the parties with a convenient mechanism for transfer of ownership under the contract between them—a particularly useful mechanism where the document of title is to be handed over only against payment.

Two things follow from what has been said above. First, a document of title of goods, unlike a document of title to land, is inherently transitory, subsisting only for so long as the goods remain in the possession of the bailee by whom the document was issued. Secondly, a document of title serves no useful purpose in the hands of the transferee unless he intends to deal with the goods while they are still in the bailee's possession. If his intention is to take delivery himself from the bailee he has no need of a document of title at all; indeed, his insistence on being provided with a document of title may prove a positive hindrance to his ability to collect the goods. Despite this,

[2] However, in contrast to a negotiable instrument the transferee does not in general acquire any better title than his transferor.

many buyers of goods to be shipped do insist on a bill of lading when their interests would be better served by a non-negotiable sea waybill, a point to which I shall return later.

What documents are documents of title?

(1) *At common law*

Before the waters became muddied by statute, the concept of a document of title was tolerably clear. It was a document which by the established custom of merchants conferred on the holder control of the goods, in that it embodied the bailee's undertaking to keep the goods for the holder and deliver them up to him or to his order.[3] Accordingly possession of the document conferred on the holder constructive possession of the goods themselves, for the bailee was in effect attorning to the holder in advance.

It will be apparent from this description that to qualify as a document of title in the sense described above at least three conditions had to be satisfied. First, the document had to be issued *by the bailee.* A document addressed *to* the bailee by the bailor requiring him to deliver the goods to a third party (*e.g.* a buyer from the bailor) would not qualify as a document of title, for it did not embody any undertaking by the bailee, whose duty thus remained owed exclusively to the original bailor. Secondly, the document had to relate to identified goods, for otherwise it would do no more than give the holder a personal right to delivery of goods of the description, quantity, etc., referred to in it. Thirdly, it had to be a document which by the custom of merchants was transferable by delivery, with any necessary indorsement, so that the bailee's duty was owed to the current holder.

Only one document of title was recognized at common law, namely the shipped bill of lading, a document issued by the sea carrier acknowledging receipt of the goods on board the vessel and evidencing the terms of carriage. In theory new documents of title could be created by the custom of merchants, but the courts steadfastly refused to go beyond the bill of lading and to accept mercantile customs as to other documents fulfilling a similar function, in particular ship's delivery orders and dock and warehouse warrants.[4]

[3] The undertaking could be express or implied, *e.g.* from issue of a delivery order by the carrier or other bailee addressed to his own ship or warehouse authorising release of the goods to the holder of the delivery order.

[4] *Farina* v. *Home* (1846) 16 M. & W. 119; *Zwinger* v. *Samuda* (1817) 7 Taunt. 265. The explanation given by Blackburn for the special position of the bill of lading was that while a buyer of goods afloat who took the bill of lading would find it physically difficult to seek out the master of the ship and get his attornment, no such impediment confronted the buyer of goods on land who took a delivery order

(2) *The Factors Act 1889*

Had the courts not been so rigid in their concept of the document of title, many problems that now face us might have been avoided. But judicial reluctance to look beyond the bill of lading led to the passing of a series of Factors Acts, culminating in the Act of 1889, section 1(4) of which defines a document of title as including:

> "any bill of lading, dock warrant, warehouse-keeper's certificate and warrant or order for the delivery of goods and any other document used in the ordinary course of business as proof of the possession or control of goods, or as authorising or purporting to authorise, either by endorsement or by delivery, the possessor of the document to transfer or receive goods thereby represented."

Now the problem with this definition is that it extends the concept of a document of title so as to embrace not merely a delivery *undertaking* issued *by* the carrier or warehouseman but a delivery *order* addressed *to* him by the shipper or other bailor and given to the consignee or other transferee of the goods. No doubt such an order is sometimes referred to by merchants as a document of title, but it is important to appreciate that, being issued by the bailor instead of by the bailee, it differs from a bill of lading or dock or warehouse warrant in one vital respect, in that it embodies no undertaking of any kind on the part of the bailee. Hence transfer of the delivery order does not by itself confer on the transferee any rights against the bailee, whose duty continues to be owed to his bailor unless and until (a) the transferee of the delivery order acquires legal title to the goods[5] or (b) the bailee attorns to the transferee by counter-signing the delivery order or otherwise acknowledging that he now holds the goods for the transferee.[6]

(3) *Statutory dock and warehouse warrants*

To complete the picture, I should draw your attention to the fact that various undertakings incorporated by private Act of Parliament are empowered by the Act concerned to issue warrants for goods which are transferable by delivery and indorsement and confer on the holder the right to delivery of the goods they represent.[7] Such warrants are therefore made documents of title in the common law sense.

issued by a wharfinger or warehouse (Blackburn, *A Treatise on the Effect of the Contract of Sale* (2nd ed.), p. 415). The explanation is unconvincing, for a land-based representative of the shipping company or charterer could equally well attorn to the buyer in respect of goods on board the ship.

[5] *Biddle* v. *Bond* (1865) 6 B. & S. 225; *Batut* v. *Hartley* (1872) 26 L.T. 968.

[6] See above, p. 9.

[7] See *Benjamin's Sale of Goods* (3rd ed.), para. 1481.

Effect of transfer of document of title to specific goods

The transfer of a bill of lading or statutory warrant entitles the transferee to claim possession of the goods from the bailee but does not by itself create privity of contract between the transferee and the bailee. However, at common law a new contract is readily implied as the result of the transferee's presentation of a bill of lading and acceptance of the goods, for in releasing the goods to him the shipowner gives up his lien for freight, so that by implication the transferee assumes responsibility for the freight, whilst on the other side the shipowner, having received or become entitled to collect freight from the transferee, is taken to have agreed to hold the goods for the transferee upon the terms of the bill of lading and thus to accept responsibility to the transferee for their loss or damage, whether caused before or after the transfer of the bill of lading.[8] Further, by the Bills of Lading Act 1855, s.1, every consignee or indorsee of the bill of lading to whom the property in the goods has passed acquires all the rights, and becomes subject to all the liabilities, created by the contract embodied in the bill of lading as if that contract has been made with him. Where section 1 applies it is unnecessary to show the existence of a new contract *in fact*, as would be required at common law.[9] On the other hand, the statutory provision operates only where the property in the goods has passed to the consignee or indorsee concerned.

Documents of title to quasi-specific goods

I now turn to consider the position of the parties where a document of title is issued which does not fully identify the goods but merely refers to an unsegregated part of a larger bulk held by the bailee. Here it is necessary to distinguish the true document of title (*i.e.* the bill of lading or statutory warrant) from the pseudo-document of title created by the Factors Act, such as a delivery order issued by the bailor instead of by the bailee.

(1) *True document of title*

A shipper who furnishes the requisite information in writing to the carrier is entitled to a bill of lading which shows the leading marks necessary for the identification of the goods, if these are stamped on the goods or their containers or coverings, and the number of packages or pieces or the quantity or weight.[10] Similarly, in the absence of agreement or usage to the contrary the buyer of goods under a contract which places responsibility for shipment on the seller is

[8] *Brandt* v. *Liverpool, Brazil & River Plate Steam Navigation Co. Ltd.* [1924] 1 K.B. 575; *Sanders* v. *Vanzeller* (1843) 4 Q.B. 260; *Cock* v. *Taylor* (1811) 13 East 399.
[9] *Ibid.*
[10] Hague-Visby Rules, art. III, r. 3.

entitled to a bill of lading which identifies the goods on board the vessel so as to make them distinguishable from the rest of the cargo.[11] To fulfil its true function as a document of title the bill of lading should identify the goods in this way. Nevertheless it is common for traders to accept bills of lading covering only an unidentified part of a ship's cargo, particularly where it is bulk cargo such as iron ore, grain or oil. In such a case, a transferee of the bill of lading acquires neither ownership nor constructive possession of any part of the cargo, for identification is necessary both for the transfer of property[12] and for a true attornment by the carrier.[13] All that the transferee acquires is a personal right against the carrier to deliver at the port of discharge goods of the requisite description, quantity, etc.[14]

(2) *Documents of title issued by the bailor*

Seller has 100 cases of Chateau Montrose claret in store in Keeper's warehouse. He contracts to sell 40 cases to Buyer and gives Buyer a delivery order addressed to Keeper requiring him to release to Buyer or his order 40 cases of Chateau Montrose claret. For the purpose of the Factors Act this is a document of title. But what a peculiar animal it is! It does not identify the goods, so that neither property nor constructive possession passes to Buyer. Moreover, since it is not a document issued by Keeper, its delivery to Buyer confers on him no rights of any kind against Keeper, who can only become Buyer's bailee by electing to attorn to him. What, then, is the significance of this strange document of title, which does not even give the holder a personal right of action against the bailee?

We are indebted to Mr. Andrew Nicol for raising the issue in this stark form in a thought-provoking article several years ago in the Modern Law Review.[15] In that article, Mr. Nicol examined three cases in which a transferee of the delivery order was held entitled to sue the issuer of the order, or the warehouseman assenting to it, in conversion for refusing to release from the bulk held or controlled by him the unidentified part covered by the delivery order.

(a) *Capital and Counties Bank Ltd.* v. *Warriner*[16]

S agreed to sell to B part of a quantity of wheat held for S in W's warehouse, and sent a transfer order direct to W instructing him to make the necessary transfer to B. W entered the transfer in his books

[11] *Re Reinhold & Co.* (1896) 12 T.L.R. 422.
[12] Sale of Goods Act 1979, s.16.
[13] See above, p. 11.
[14] See below, pp. 65 *et seq*.
[15] "The Passing of Property in Part of a Bulk" (1979) 42 M.L.R. 129.
[16] (1896) 1 Com.Cas. 314.

and notified B that he had received from S the transfer order in B's favour. The part which was the subject of the contract of sale was not separated from the bulk held by W. Subsequently W issued to B two warrants recording that wheat to the given quantities was held to B's order. B indorsed and delivered these warrants to the plaintiff bank by way of pledge to secure an overdraft. B stopped payment and S sought to recover from W so much of the wheat as had not been delivered to B, on the ground that until separation from the bulk S remained the owner of the wheat and the bank did not acquire any rights to it. The bank relied on the Factors Act 1889, s.9, contending that S as well as W was estopped from denying the bank's title.

Mathew J. upheld the bank's contention. Under the Factors Act, s.9, the bank acquired a pledge right effective against S and overriding any lien he might otherwise have possessed. Section 9 was not confined to specific goods and in any event S was estopped from disputing the bank's title.

(b) Ant. Jurgens Margerinefabrieken v. *Louis Dreyfus*[17]

S agreed to sell to B a quantity of mowra seed forming part of a larger consignment being shipped to Hamburg. B gave S a cheque for the mowra seed and received in exchange two delivery orders addressed to S's Hamburg house which B indorsed over to his sub-buyer, SB, against the price payable by SB on the sub-sale. B's cheque having been dishonoured, S instructed its Hamburg house not to deliver the seed to SB, who thereupon instituted proceedings against B.

It was held that although the goods were not specific the plaintiffs were entitled to succeed since the delivery orders were documents of title which had been "transferred" within the Factors Act, s.10, by S to B and re-transferred by B to SB, who thus acquired rights to the seed overriding S's rights as unpaid vendor.

(c) D.F. Mount Ltd. v. *Jay & Jay (Provisions) Ltd.*[18]

S agreed to sell to B a quantity of peaches forming part of a consignment lying at W's wharf. B agreed to sell part of this quantity to SB for sub-sale to his customers. S gave B two delivery orders in B's favour addressed to W. B then issued its own delivery orders in favour of SB who indorsed them in favour of his own buyers, the plaintiffs. The plaintiffs subsequently contracted to sell the peaches

[17] [1914] 3 K.B. 40.
[18] [1960] 1 Q.B. 159.

back to SB, and issued delivery orders to him but cancelled these when SB failed to pay the repurchase price. Meanwhile B, having failed to obtain payment from SB on the original sub-sale, cancelled their contract with him and wrote to W requesting cancellation of the delivery orders in SB's favour. The plaintiffs claimed the right to the peaches, whilst the defendant, B, asserted its rights as an unpaid seller.

The plaintiffs' claim under the Sale of Goods Act 1893, s.25(2) (similar in terms to the Factors Act, s.9), was upheld, the judge holding that the subsection was not confined to specific goods and effectively overrode B's rights as unpaid seller.

Mr. Nicol argued that these cases were wrongly decided since they either overlooked the Sale of Goods Act, s.16, or erroneously dismissed that section as irrelevant to the transferee's right to invoke the Factors Act, s.9, and the Sale of Goods Act, s.25(2). My own view is that the decisions were correct, since whilst a claim based on ownership would have failed for want of ascertainment under section 16, there is no reason why a seller who issues or a warehouseman who assents to a delivery order should not be exposed to a personal action in conversion for refusal to release the requisite quantity of goods. Identification of the goods is not necessary for this purpose; the holder of the delivery order is entitled, by contract or estoppel, to receive goods from an identified bulk, and his right to possession is infringed if release of goods from the bulk is refused. Of the two cases relied on by Mr. Nicol as implicitly denying an action for conversion based on estoppel, one had nothing to do with conversion at all, being an action by the seller for the price,[19] whilst in the other the court, having held that section 16 debarred a claim based on ownership, would have given judgment on the basis of an attornment if it had been satisfied that the bailee had in fact assented to the delivery order.[20]

If, then, goods belonging to S are held in W's warehouse and S issues a delivery order to B for an unidentified part of the goods,[21] what does possession of this delivery order do for B or his transferee, SB? From the various cases we can draw the following conclusions:

(1) As holder of the delivery order, B has a right to require S to procure W's acceptance of the order by the due delivery date at latest, for otherwise S will not be fulfilling his duty as seller to give B

[19] *Healy* v. *Howlett & Sons* [1917] 1 K.B. 337.

[20] *Laurie & Morewood* v. *Dudin & Sons* [1926] 1 K.B. 223.

[21] B is not obliged to accept such an order unless he has agreed to do so, expressly or by implication.

a right to possession.[22] W's failure to accept the order thus entitles B to sue S for damages for breach of contract or alternatively for conversion. B has no claim against W until the latter's acceptance of the order. Until segregation of the goods in such a manner as to constitute an irrevocable appropriation, W's acceptance does not constitute an attornment so as to give B constructive possession of the goods but merely confers on B a personal right to delivery through estoppel (or through a new contract, if one can be established), a right that would be converted into a right to prove in competition with other creditors if W became bankrupt before appropriation.

(2) If B makes over the delivery order to SB, *e.g.* under a sub-sale or by way of pledge, SB, though having no contractual relationship with S, is entitled to sue S in conversion if S fails to procure W's acceptance of the delivery order. SB has no claim against W, even if W had previously assented to the order in favour of B, unless and until W attorns to SB. Upon such attornment SB acquires the same rights against W as B had in case (1).

(3) In the conditions laid down by sections 25 and 47(2), SB's rights against S under (2) above prevail over S's rights as unpaid vendor and are therefore exercisable even though S could have relied on his continued ownership and/or lien or right of stoppage in transit to withhold possession from B. Thus although the two statutory provisions are in most cases invoked for the purpose of giving the claimant title to identified goods overriding the original seller's title, they are not confined to proprietary claims to identified goods but can equally be invoked by the holder of a purely personal claim to quasi-specific goods so as to prevent that claim being defeated by a possessory right enjoyed by S against B.

(4) If two or more delivery orders are issued by S to buyers in succession, B1 and B2, each acquires the rights against S described in (1) above. No question of priority arises, for *ex hypothesi* the goods are not identified, so that both claims are purely personal.

[22] *Smith* v. *Chance* (1819) 2 B. & Ald. 753. As seller S has a duty to deliver the goods in accordance with the terms of the contract of sale (Sale of Goods Act 1979, s.27), and there is no delivery unless and until W acknowledges to B that he holds the goods on B's behalf (*ibid.* s.29(4)). But a quasi-attornment by W to B in respect of an unsegregated part of the bulk held by him will suffice to satisfy S's delivery obligation, even though constructive possession does not pass to B, if under the express or implied terms of the contract it is for B to arrange with W for withdrawal of the contract quantity from the bulk and its collection by B or delivery by W (see Sale of Goods Act 1979, s.29(1)). This is implicit in the decision in *Sterns Ltd.* v. *Vickers Ltd.* [1923] 1 K.B. 78 that in such a case the risk passes to the buyer, a ruling which presupposes that it was not the duty of the seller in that case to procure segregation and a true attornment.

Hence whilst the issue or transfer of a delivery order relating to an unidentified part of a bulk has no proprietary effects at all, the status of the delivery order as a document of title for the purposes of the Factors Act and the Sale of Goods Act makes it more powerful than a mere written authority by S to W to release the goods to B. In particular, B's rights against S can be transferred by mere delivery of the delivery order with any necessary indorsement, and this may be effective to give SB a personal right to possession against S when, by virtue of the terms of the contract of sale or the exercise of a lien or right of stoppage in transit, S could legitimately have withheld possession from B.

2. DEALINGS IN GOODS IN SEA TRANSIT

Goods shipped f.o.b. and c.i.f.

Under the strict f.o.b. contract the seller has no responsibility for arranging the contract of sea carriage. His duty is simply to put on board a vessel properly nominated by the buyer goods answering the contract description. Thereafter his responsibility ceases, property and risk passing to the buyer on shipment.[23] Frequently, however, it is found convenient for the f.o.b. seller to make the shipping arrangements as the buyer's agent. This work being extra to what is covered by the f.o.b. price, the seller will charge a commission and his responsibility for the transportation arrangements, being in the capacity of agent rather than of seller, is limited to the exercise of reasonable care.

In the case of a c.i.f. contract, it is the responsibility of the seller, as a term of the contract, either to ship goods in conformity with the contract at his own expense consigned to the contractual port of discharge or to purchase afloat goods so shipped. Whichever of these two methods is adopted, risk prima facie passes as from the time of shipment but the property does not usually pass until delivery of the bill of lading to the buyer at the earliest[24]; and if the buyer fails to pay on such delivery the transfer of property to him will generally be further deferred until payment.[25]

[23] *Carlos Federspiel & Co. SA* v. *Charles Twigg & Co. Ltd.* [1957] 1 Lloyd's Rep. 240; *Stock* v. *Inglis* (1884) 12 Q.B.D. 564, *per* Brett M.R., at p. 573, affirmed (1885) 19 App.Cas. 263; *The Parchim* [1918] A.C. 157. Where the seller undertakes responsibility for shipment as the buyer's agent and reserves the right of disposal, *e.g.* by taking the bill of lading to his own order, the transfer of the property is deferred (Sale of Goods Act 1979, s.19(1), (2)) but risk still passes on shipment (*Williams* v. *Cohen* (1871) 25 L.T. 300, *per* Bramwell B., at p. 303).

[24] *The Miramichi* [1915] P. 71.

[25] *Ibid.*; *Ginzberg* v. *Barrow Haematitte Steel Co. Ltd.* [1966] 1 Lloyd's Rep. 343.

Transfer of the bill of lading

Delivery of the bill of lading and other shipping documents enables the buyer to deal with the goods in transit by transfer of the bill of lading, with any necessary indorsement, whether by way of sale to his sub-purchaser, pledge to his bank or otherwise. A buyer who as consignee or indorsee of the bill of lading acquires the property in the goods upon or by reason of such consignment or indorsement obtains a statutory transfer of all the seller's rights against the carrier as if the contract contained in the bill of lading had been made with the buyer.[26]

Without the bill of lading the buyer would not be a statutory assignee of the seller's rights and any action against the carrier in respect of the goods would have to be based in tort for negligence or conversion and would be admissible only if the carrier's wrongful act or omission took place after the buyer had acquired ownership or possession[27] (including constructive possession by attornment[28]) or at least a personal right against the carrier by virtue of contract or quasi-attornment in respect of an undivided part of a bulk.[29] Where the loss or damage occurs while the seller still owns the goods and holds the bill of lading the buyer cannot sue (in the absence of a contract with or attornment by the carrier) unless he obtains an assignment of the seller's right of action or the seller brings an action himself against the carrier. In the latter event the seller would be accountable to the buyer for any sum recovered in the action.[30] However, it has been said that the seller does not hold the claim itself on trust for the buyer and cannot be compelled to sue the carrier for the benefit of the buyer.[31] If this be right, a buyer faced with a recalcitrant seller who refuses either to assign the claim or to sue himself is deprived of all remedy. I have suggested elsewhere that this does not represent English law and that the seller must be taken

[26] Bills of Lading Act 1855, s.1. The interpretation of the section is not free from difficulty. Literally construed it would rarely apply, since the property in the goods passes by virtue of the contract of sale rather than upon or by reason of the consignment or indorsement of the bill of lading as such, and the bill of lading does not usually contain the terms of the contract of carriage, it merely evidences those terms. For a detailed analysis, see *Benjamin's Sale of Goods* (3rd ed.), para. 1456.

[27] *Leigh & Sillivan Ltd.* v. *Aliakmon Shipping Co. Ltd. (The Aliakmon)* [1986] A.C. 785. See below, p. 71. An equitable owner cannot sue in his own name but must join the legal owner, as plaintiff if he is willing or as defendant if he is not (*ibid. per* Lord Brandon at p. 910).

[28] In the case of attornment the buyer would have an alternative claim for breach of bailment, as was explicitly recognised by Lord Brandon in *The Aliakmon* (n. 27 above) at p. 818.

[29] The carrier being estopped from disputing that he held the lost or damaged goods for the buyer, the latter has the same personal remedies against the carrier as if there had been a true attornment.

[30] *The Albazero* [1977] A.C. 774, *per* Lord Diplock at pp. 845–846.

[31] *Ibid.*

to hold the claim itself, and not merely the fruits of the claim, on trust for the buyer.[32]

Where the bill of lading is obtained by the buyer then in theory, the system should work perfectly, in accordance with well-established and tolerably straightforward principles. If only life were so simple! But business practices are not readily confined within a legal strait-jacket, and three factors may introduce serious complications: the shipment of goods under a bill of lading which does not identify them so as to make them distinguishable from other cargo of the same description; the fact that all too often the bill of lading does not arrive until after the goods, thus largely defeating the purpose of its issue; and the archaic habit of issuing original bills of lading in a set of three, each of which may come into different hands. It is these three factors to which I shall devote the rest of this evening's lecture.

(1) Shipment of Quasi-Specific Goods

The practice

As stated earlier, a buyer is prima facie entitled to a bill of lading which identifies the goods on board the vessel, marking them off from other cargo of like description. But in the case of bulk cargo, such as oil or grain, which is not packed, boxed or crated but simply poured as an undivided mass into the ship's hold, segregation of individual consignments is considered neither convenient nor necessary; indeed, when there may be as many as 2,000 bills of lading covering a single shipment it would be impossible to provide separate storage tanks for each consignment. Hence the parties frequently agree, by express terms, usage or course of dealing, that it will suffice for the seller to tender a bill of lading covering an unidentified part of the total cargo.

Effect of non-segregation on the buyer

Failure to segregate the buyer's goods weakens the force of the bill of lading to an extent that is probably not generally realized. Since the goods are not ascertained within section 16 of the Sale of Goods Act, property does not pass to the buyer, nor does he acquire constructive possession, prior to appropriation to his contract. In consequence, the transfer to him of the bill of lading is not by itself effective as an assignment of the seller's rights under the contract of carriage, for under section 1 of the Bills of Lading Act 1855 such transfer occurs in favour of the consignee or indorsee of the bill only if he has acquired the property in the goods. Hence if the goods are

[32] R. M. Goode, "Ownership and Obligation in Commercial Transactions," (1987) 103 L.Q.R. 433 at pp. 456–458.

lost or damaged in transit through the fault of the carrier, the buyer has no claim in contract except where he can establish a new contract with or an attornment by the carrier.[33]

Worse is to come. In *The Aliakmon*[34] the House of Lords, overruling *The Irene's Success*[35] and restoring the authority of the earlier decision in *The Wear Breeze* [36] has reaffirmed the principle that no action for negligent loss of or damage to the goods while in transit lies against the carrier except at the suit of a person who at the time of the loss or damage had either a proprietary or a possessory title to them.[37] Accordingly a buyer who cannot show that the loss or damage occurred after the goods intended for him had been separated from the bulk has no claim in tort for negligence.

The upshot of all this is that one who takes a bill of lading covering an unidentified part of a bulk cargo may find that if the cargo is lost or damaged through the negligence of the ship he has no right to sue the carrier either in contract or in tort and is entirely dependent on the co-operation of his seller in the pursuit of proceedings.

The position of the sellers of commingled goods

Where oil or other bulk cargo, wet or dry, belonging to different sellers becomes commingled on shipment, accidentally or by consent, in such a way that the mixture cannot be separated, the various sellers become owners in common of the mass in the proportion of their respective contributions[38] and bear rateably any loss resulting from damage or wastage of the cargo in transit. The same principle applies where goods shipped by a seller on board a vessel become commingled with those of the owner of the vessel. The position where the commingling takes place without consent through the intentional act of one of the parties was exhaustively examined by Staughton J. in *The Ypatianna*,[39] where the learned judge, after a survey of authorities going back to Justinian, rejected the proposition that the entirety of the cargo was forfeited to the innocent party and

[33] See above, pp. 10, 63.

[34] [1986] A.C. 785, affirming the decision of the Court of Appeal [1985] Q.B. 350.

[35] *Schiffahrt und Kohlen GmbH* v. *Chelsea Maritime Ltd. (The Irene's Success)* [1982] 2 Q.B. 481.

[36] *Margarine Union GmbH* v. *Cambay Prince Steamship Co. Ltd. (The Wear Breeze)* [1969] 1 Q.B. 219.

[37] For a penetrating analysis of this aspect of the decision, see B. S. Markesinis, "An Expanding Tort Law—The Price of a Rigid Contract Law" (1987) 103 L.Q.R. 354 at pp. 384 *et seq.*

[38] *Spence* v. *Union Marine Insurance Ltd.* (1868) L.R. 3 C.P. 427; *Sandeman & Sons* v. *Tyzack & Branfort Steamship Co. Ltd.* [1913] A.C. 680. This form of admixture is known as *confusio*, or confusion, and in giving the various contributors co-ownership in the proportion of their respective contributions English law follows the Roman law doctrine of *confusio*.

[39] *Indian Oil Corp. Ltd.* v. *Greenstone Shipping S.A. (The Ypatianna)* [1987] 2 Lloyd's Rep. 286. See further p. 90, below.

concluded that the rule went no further than allowing the innocent party to claim what he had contributed, any doubt as to the quantity of his contribution being resolved in his favour and any loss resulting from the admixture or from diminution of the cargo, whether through wastage or otherwise, being borne by the guilty party.

Wastage in transit is inevitable for most types of bulk cargo and may result from a variety of causes, including evaporation, dehydration, adhesion to pipes and tanks, and viscosity rendering liquid cargo unpumpable. The rule that loss resulting from wastage is borne rateably applies only in the relations between the co-owners *inter se* and does not concern the carrier, who is not obliged to apportion the cargo rateably[40] and may deliver to each consignee the full quantity shipped by him, even though this throws the whole loss on the consignee who is the last to take delivery.[41] In the absence of fault the carrier is protected by article 4(2)(m) of the Hague-Visby Rules against a claim for the shortfall.[42] Whether the consignee who is left with an under-delivery can recover from the other consignees either such money sum or such part of the cargo delivered to them as will ensure rateable distribution of the loss is doubtful.[43] On principle such recovery should be allowed in order to give effect to the rateable allocation of loss and to prevent unjust enrichment.

(2) The Problem of the Delayed Bill of Lading[44]

I now turn to an even more troublesome matter, the failure of the bill of lading to move at a sufficient speed to accommodate dealings in the goods while they are still afloat.

Reasons for the delay

The failure of a bill of lading to arrive in time to fulfil its function as a document of title may be due to any one or more of a number of

[40] Though he is presumably entitled to do so.

[41] *Grange & Co.* v. *Taylor* (1904) 9 Com.Cas. 223, (1904) 20 T.L.R. 386, a decision concerning the consignment of grain some of which was unsound. As pointed out by Bingham J. in that case, to require the shipowner to separate out the sound from the unsound cargo would impose an enormous burden on him, since the sorting would require considerable labour and the shipowner would have to defer delivery to any consignee until he had discharged and sorted the entire cargo. How, where and when could he do this?

[42] For an excellent discussion of the various causes of wastage (*freinte de route*) and decisions thereon in various jurisdictions, see William Tetley, *Marine Cargo Claims* (3rd ed.), Chap. 12.

[43] See *The Ypatianna*, above, *per* Staughton J. at p. 288.

[44] See R. M. Wiseman, "Transaction Chains in North Sea Oil Cargoes." (1984) 2 J.E.R.L. 134; F.L. de May "Bills of Lading Problems in the Oil Trade: Documentary Credit Aspects" (1984) 2 J.E.R.L. 197; Alan Urbach, "The Bill of Lading: Who Owns the Cargo You Have Just Bought?" [1983/84] 12 O.G.L.T.R. 267.

factors. First, ships have become ever faster and their transit times reduced. Secondly, the bill of lading is not issued until after the ship has sailed. It is the last document in the export transaction but the first in the import transaction, so that it is the document governed by the tightest time constraint. Thirdly, delay may occur because payment is to be made under a confirmed letter of credit, so that the seller, having obtained the bill of lading, has to present it to the confirming bank in his own country, which then examines the documents and transmits them to the issuing bank in the buyer's country, which in turn examines them before passing them on to the buyer. Even if no allowance is made for postal delays, for documents left on a busy executive's desk or for sub-sales by the original buyer, this transmission chain will in many cases take a longer time to complete than the voyage of the ship. Fourthly, the paperwork may be delayed by a multiplicity of bills of lading. In the case of general cargo, there may be as many as 2,000 bills covering the cargo in a single vessel! Finally, the chain may be lengthened by resales. This is a particularly common occurrence in the case of bulk cargo such as oil, which is the subject of intensive trading on the futures market by traders who buy not for physical delivery but by way of hedge or speculation, so that a single cargo may be sold and resold no less than 40 times before the ship reaches its destinations, many such transactions taking place before the oil is shipped or even before it has been produced. Since payment along the chain is often due near-simultaneously, and letters of credit may well be involved, it is obviously impossible for the bill of lading to move down the chain in the relatively short time the cargo is afloat.

Consequences of the delay

If the parties were not to find some method of short-circuiting the normal documentary procedures, the delay in arrival of the bill of lading could have serious consequences. The importer, with orders to fulfil, might find himself in the frustrating position of seeing his goods at the docks without being able to collect them. The shipper could incur heavy charges for demurrage and storage at the port of discharge. The default in delivery down the chain would cause a string of claims resulting in cascading liability as each party sought to recover not only his own direct loss but an indemnity against liability incurred to his buyer. Finally, there could be serious port congestion if the cargo was not able to be unloaded.

The indemnity system

To break this logjam, traders have had to resort to the use of letters of indemnity as a temporary substitute for the missing bill of lading. It is now not uncommon to find express provisions in contracts of sale, and in documentary credits opened pursuant to such contracts, permitting the seller to tender to his buyer or to the issuing or confirming bank a letter of indemnity, in a form prescribed or approved by the buyer or bank, in lieu of a bill of lading so as to obtain payment without being held up pending arrival of the bill. The seller is required to pass on the bill of lading when this reaches his hands, and upon his doing so the indemnity ceases to have effect.

There are in fact two distinct indemnities involved: the indemnity given by each seller in the chain to the party (buyer or bank) to whom he has to present the shipping documents in exchange for payment; and the indemnity required by the carrier before he will release the goods to the last buyer in the chain.

A typical procedure is as follows. The original seller who has shipped the goods and is awaiting the bill of lading telexes the ship's agent at the port of discharge requesting delivery of the goods to the buyer's order without production of the bill of lading. In his telex the seller agrees to indemnify the carrier against all loss, damage and liability, to provide bail in the event of the vessel's arrest and to deliver up the bill of lading to the carrier as soon as it has arrived, in which event the seller's liability on the indemnity is to end. The buyer will then telex the ship's agent directing release of the goods to *his* buyer, and so on down the chain, so that the ship's agent ends up with the original seller's telexed indemnity plus a sheaf of telexes from which he is able to identify the last buyer in the chain. When this buyer presents himself, the shipping company will require a separate letter of indemnity from him, and if unsure of his financial standing may also require that this be counter-signed by a bank.

Meanwhile, each seller in the chain has to furnish a comparable letter of indemnity to the party (buyer or bank) from whom he seeks payment against the documents, such indemnity containing a warranty that the seller issuing it has marketable title to the cargo free and clear of any lien or encumbrance and the full right and authority to transfer such title and deliver the cargo to the buyer. In the result, there is a string of matching indemnities running from the first seller through the chain to the last buyer. Eventually, the original seller gets his hands on the bill of lading and passes this down the chain, each letter of indemnity becoming void when the recipient of it acquires the bill of lading. Finally, the bill of lading reaches the last buyer, who delivers it to the carrier, thus extinguishing his own indemnity to the carrier.

It will be apparent that in agreeing to release the goods without production of a bill of lading the carrier runs a considerable risk, for it if transpires that the person collecting the goods had no title to them the carrier incurs a liability to the true owner for his direct loss and may also have to indemnify him against claims by his buyer, which in turn may include claims by the latter's sub-buyer, etc., so that there is a cascading liability all of which ultimately falls on to the hapless carrier. It is for this reason that the P & I Clubs do not offer insurance cover against such risks and many banks refuse to counter-sign letters of indemnity.

Title conflicts

The statement made above as to the carrier's liability to the true owner presupposes that we can identify the true owner—using the term in this context to denote one who has either title or the best right to possession—and also that we can establish that the delivery by the carrier infringes the true owner's proprietary or possessory rights. This task is slightly complicated by the practice above referred to of taking a bill of lading covering an unidentified part of the bulk on board the vessel. At that stage, the holder of the bill of lading cannot claim to be the owner of anything; he has merely a personal right to require the carrier to release to him goods of the description, quantity, etc., set out in the bill of lading. If, when the bill is passed down the line and presented by the ultimate buyer to the carrier, there is sufficient cargo of the contract description on board to cover the bill of lading, there is no problem. The presenter simply takes delivery of the quantity specified in the bill. However, the earlier release to the wrong party obviously means that there will not be enough cargo on board to satisfy all the bills of lading, and the latecomers may find either that there is nothing left for them at all or that what is left falls short of the quantity to which they are entitled. In this case, they can sue the carrier for conversion. The last person to present his bill will usually have a concurrent right of action in contract, for the effect of prior deliveries under the other bills of lading will be that *his* goods will have become ascertained by exhaustion,[45] so that section 16 of the Sale of Goods Act 1979 is satisfied and (if there are no other unfulfilled conditions for the transfer of property to him) he will acquire title, thus enabling him to sue on the bill of lading under section 1 of the Bills of Lading Act 1855. If the carrier is insolvent, the disappointed holder of the bill of lading will be left to prove in the bankruptcy as an unsecured creditor. He will no longer have a claim against his seller on the indemnity, for that will have been extinguished when his seller delivered the bill of lading. So in this particular game it is very much a case of first come, first served.

What happens if a seller, S, makes a fraudulent double sale of the same consignment, to B1 and B2 respectively, gives B1 an indemnity and on subsequently acquiring the bill of lading indorses this to B2? Who wins, B1 or B2? And what is the position of the carrier?

[45] *Wait & James* v. *Midland Bank* (1926) 31 Com.Cas. 172; *Karlshamns Oljefabriker* v. *Eastport Navigation Corp.* [1982] 1 All E.R. 208.

The contest between B1 and B2

In principle, priority goes to the first to acquire title; but in certain conditions this order is reversed as the result of some applicable exception to the *nemo dat* rule. The following examples will illustrate these points.

(1) *Seller sells to B2 after passing title to B1*

The transfer of title from S to B1 does not depend on delivery of the bill of lading as such; it passes under the contract of sale at the time intended by the parties.[46] Of course, S may have given instructions to the carrier that the bill of lading was to be made out to his order, thus raising a presumption that he intended to reserve a right of disposal,[47] but on the assumption that the goods have become identified and that S intended title to pass to B1 on or before shipment, the starting position is that S has nothing to transfer to B2 at the time he hands over the bill of lading. B1 will already have acquired not only title but also constructive possession, since S's delivery of the goods to the carrier consigned to B1 is prima facie delivery to B1,[48] the carrier becoming B1's agent. It would seem to follow that by subsequently issuing a bill of lading in favour of S without B1's authority, the carrier is committing a conversion of B1's goods. Though the effect of the carrier's unlawful attornment is to divest B1 of constructive possession and vest this in S, he will not be able to pass a good title to B2 as a seller in possession under the Factors Act, s.8, or the Sale of Goods Act 1979, s.24, for those sections apparently do not apply where the seller was in possession at the time of the first sale but lost possession before regaining it at the time of the second sale.[49] In other words, they are confined to cases where the seller either had possession at the time of the first sale and maintained it continuously until delivery of the bill of lading to the second buyer or never had it at the time of the first sale but acquired possession by the time of the second sale. So B2 cannot invoke this exception to the *nemo dat* rule, and no other exception appears applicable. Even if we supposed that S were a mercantile agent, thus bringing section 2 of the Factors Act 1889 into consideration, that section applies only to a disposition by a mercantile agent in possession *with the consent of the owner*, whereas in the case in point B1, having acquired constructive possession, has not consented to this passing to S.

[46] Sale of Goods Act 1979, s.17.

[47] *Ibid.* s.19(2).

[48] *Ibid.* s.32(1).

[49] *Mitchell* v. *Jones* (1905) 24 N.Z.L.R. 932; *Worcester Works Finance Ltd.* v. *Cooden Engineering Co. Ltd.* [1972] 1 Q.B. 210.

(2) *Seller sells to B2 before passing title to B1*

The case here postulated is that S contracts first with B1, consigning the goods to him, but has not passed title to B1 before transferring title to B2 and indorsing the bill of lading to him. In this situation B2 wins because he has both ownership and constructive possession. B1's contractual right to acquire the goods[50] is displaced by the transfer of property to B2. In addition, as in the first example, B1 loses constructive possession, since by issuing the bill of lading to S the carrier attorns to him and any subsequent holder.

(3) *Neither B1 nor B2 acquires title during the transit*

This would typically occur where both contracts of sale related to an undivided part of a bulk cargo. In this situation, and assuming that the only condition precedent to the transfer of title under either contract is ascertainment of the goods, title passes to the buyer to whom the goods are first appropriated.

The position of the carrier

As I have pointed out, if a carrier who receives goods consigned to B1 subsequently attorns to S or to B2 without B1's authority, he incurs a liability to B1 for conversion; and this is the case whether or not the goods intended for B1 have been segregated or B1 has acquired legal title, for as B1's deemed bailee under section 32(1) of the Sale of Goods Act the carrier is estopped from disputing either that he has segregated the goods or that B1 is entitled to possession.

(3) Issue of Bills in a Set

The problem

It is still common for bills of lading to be issued in a set of three originals, each specifying the number comprised in the set and stating that "one of which being accomplished, the other shall stand void." Whatever justification may at one time have existed for issuing original bills of lading in sets has long since disappeared. The continuance of this practice, due primarily to ingrained tradition, is to be roundly condemned, for it exposes the parties to quite unnecessary risk.

The rules governing the situation where part of the set comes into the hands of B1 and the rest into the possession of B2 in that order are tolerably clear. B1 has priority and the delivery of the remaining

[50] It will be recalled that the buyer has no equitable interest in the goods prior to transfer of the legal title. See above, p. 6.

bill or bills of lading to B2 has no effect.[51] As regards the carrier, if one of the originals is presented to him and he then has no notice that any other is in different hands, he is entitled to release the goods to the presenting party and incurs no liability merely by reason of the fact that the holder of the other original has a better title.[52] In other words, the carrier is entitled to rely on the statement that when delivery has been made under one bill the others are to become void. The position is otherwise where the master is on notice that the other original is in different hands. In such a case, his proper course is to interplead, and if he releases the goods against one of the originals only he does so at his peril.[53] Where the bills are pledged in succession to different pledgees, the pledges rank in order of time.[54]

3. THE REPLACEMENT OR LOCALISATION OF BILLS OF LADING

The problems described above, coupled with a more general need to reduce the volume and movement of paper in international trade, have resulted in a growing number of studies into the feasibility of restricting, if not entirely displacing, the bill of lading as a means of transferring control of goods. Invaluable work has been done by the United Nations Economic Commission for Europe, through its Working Party on Facilitation of International Trade Procedures, by the Trade Facilitation Council of the Nordic Council (NORDIPRO), assisted by one of the world's leading experts in transport law, Professor Kurt Gronfors of the University of Gotenberg[55] and more recently by UNCITRAL, which has assumed a leading role in work in this field. In order to appreciate the legal and technical problems that are now being discussed by these bodies it may be helpful to summarise the key features of the bill of lading as a conventional transport document.

Characteristics of the bill of lading

The traditional bill of lading possesses the following features the disappearance of which may be expected to cause legal problems:

(1) It is a document, that is, a paper writing constituting a record in permanent form of the carrier's receipt of the goods and the terms of the contract of carriage.

[51] *Barber* v. *Meyerstein* (1870) L.R. 4 H.L. 317.
[52] *Glyn Mills Currie & Co.* v. *East & West India Dock Co.* (1882) 7 App.Cas. 591.
[53] *Ibid. per* Lord Blackburn at p. 611.
[54] *Barber* v. *Meyerstein,* above.
[55] For an analysis of the legal problems and possible solutions see Eric Bergsten and Roy Goode, "Legal questions and problems to be overcome," in *Trading with EDI: The Legal Issues* (ed. Thomsen and Wheble) Chapter 7. See also NORDIPRO's Special Paper No. 3, *Legal Acceptance of International Trade Data Transmitted by Electronic Means* (1983).

(2) The document carries a signature identifying the issuer of the document and authenticating its contents.
(3) The document is issued at the port of shipment.
(4) It is then physically transmitted to the consignee of the named goods at the port of destination.
(5) Production of the document to the carrier at the port of destination is required in order to secure release of the goods.
(6) Accordingly, control of the goods can be transferred by negotiation of the document.

Physical transfer of documents as the key problem

The feature that causes the greatest obstacle to the efficient transfer of goods from one country to another is the need for the physical movement of the bill of lading and related documents (commercial invoice, insurance policy or certificate, certificates of origin, quality, etc.), usually in multiple copies, from the country of export to the country of import. Production of the many documents required is time-consuming and costly,[56] the documents take up space, they are susceptible to forgery and theft and the delay in their transmission and arrival causes the most acute problems, as we have seen. If this physical movement of documents can be eliminated, much time and expense will be saved.

Elimination of the movement of documents

The search for ways of avoiding the physical transfer of the bill of lading and associated documents from one country to another has resulted in the emergence of three principal approaches to the problem. The first is to restrict the use of the bill of lading to cases where it is necessary and in other cases to issue a non-negotiable receipt for the goods which serves as a record for the shipper but does not require to be produced at the other end. The second is to preserve the traditional bill of lading but to localise it by use of a central register in which all transfers of the bill of lading would take place. The third is to recognize a document reproduced electronically at the port of *destination* and incorporating the relevant trade data transmitted electronically from the port of shipment. Electronic data processing (EDP)—also known as automated data processing (ADP)—is

[56] "An investigation in the U.S. has shown that while in 1970 on average 45 documents were required, five years later it had risen to nearly 100. Documentation and procedures are estimated to represent some 7–10 per cent. of invoice value—an unacceptably high figure" (*Creating Legal Security in Electronic Data Interchange*. A guide to the UNCID-rules. 4th special paper by NORDIPRO (1988), p. 8).

already in use to a limited extent and is attracting increasing attention.

The non-negotiable receipt

The *raison d'être* of the bill of lading is the desire of the shipper or consignee to be able to sell or pledge the goods in transit. Little purpose is served by insistence on a bill of lading where the party in whose favour it is to be issued does not wish to deal with the goods in transit but intends to take physical delivery of them at the port of arrival. Most container shipments fall into this category, yet tradition dies hard, and many parties continue to stipulate for the shipped bill of lading when they have no need of it, thereby risking the very delay that the bill of lading was originally designed to avoid.

Increasingly the sea way-bill is perceived as a sensible substitute for the bill of lading. The advantage of the sea way-bill is that it is no more than a non-negotiable receipt for the goods which evidences the shipment and incorporates by reference the terms of the contract of carriage. It is not necessary for the consignee to produce the document in order to secure the release of the goods from the carrier; all he has to do is to furnish acceptable evidence of his identity.

A form of non-negotiable receipt allied to electronic data processing was successfully developed in 1971 by Atlantic Container Line (ACL), which found that in the case of most container cargo crossing the North Atlantic the consignor and the consignee belonged to the same trading group, so that dispositions in transit never happened. Advised by Professor Gronfors, ACL created a Datafreight Receipt System, in which a conventional non-negotiable receipt in paper form is produced and issued to the shipper and in addition the information contained in the receipt is transmitted by computer to the port of arrival and reproduced in an arrival notice print-out which gives details of the time of arrival and is posted to the consignee. The electronically transmitted datafreight receipt is accepted as proof of entitlement to the goods. This system thus embodies the concept of the non-negotiable receipt but adds the notion of a separate document produced electronically at the port of destination and used by the buyer to procure release of the goods.

Localisation of the bill of lading

Recognizing the reluctance of shipping interests to depart from the traditional bill of lading, INTERTANKO and the Chase Manhattan Bank came up with an ingenious proposal, termed SeaDocs, to create a Central Registry which would hold bills of lading as agent for all interested parties. The bill of lading in traditional form would be issued to the shipper in the first instance in the usual way and would then be lodged by him with the Central Registry. When the shipper wished to transfer the bill of lading to a named consignee he would send a message to that effect to the Registry, which after confirmation back to the shipper would then telex the carrier requesting him to release the goods to the consignee. The Registry would indorse the bill of lading as agent of the shipper and thereafter hold it as agent of the consignee. Further transfers could be effected in similar fashion, the Registry indorsing on behalf of each transferor and continuing in possession as agent of the transferee. Whilst Sea-Docs reduced the movement of paper, its operation depended in the first instance on the issue of a bill of lading to the shipper and its physical delivery to the Registry, so that as regards this phase it failed to eliminate the problems currently experienced. Unhappily the pilot scheme did not lead to any support for the project, which was ultimately abandoned. It may, however, be revived.

Electronic data processing

Reference has already been made to the Datafreight Receipt System devised for ACL by Professor Gronfors. This system is based on the assumption that there will be no dealings with the goods in transit. However, there are many cases in which the buyer, though not wishing to sub-sell in transit, finds it necessary to pledge the goods to his bank to secure an advance of the price. Accordingly the next step taken by Professor Gronfors was to build a banking function into the Datafreight Receipt System so as to allow of a pledge of the goods while in transit. Professor Gronors accordingly devised for ACL what he termed a Cargo Key Receipt. Under this system, the seller/shipper signs a NODISP declaration surrendering to the buyer's bank as consignee the right to dispose of the goods in transit to the buyer. The seller is issued with a Cargo Key Receipt at the port of shipment and can use this to obtain payment from his own bank. The information contained in the receipt and associated documents (invoice, etc.) is transmitted electronically to the buyer's bank, which also gets notice of the ship's intended arrival time together with a print-out of the Cargo Key Receipt, copies being sent to the buyer. The bank then indorses the Cargo Key Receipt to its customer, the buyer, in exchange for payment and the buyer procures the goods from the carrier by producing the document. The concept of a document as the key to the goods is thus retained, but the document is not an original in the traditional legal sense, for it is not the document produced at the port of shipment but a replica printed out at the port of destination from electronically transmitted data.

For various reasons, the system has so far not proved successful, due partly to the fact that it is a closed system, partly to the reluctance of those involved to move away from traditional documents and partly to the difficulty of introducing a standardised electronic system, despite valiant efforts by the U.S. National Committee on International Trade Procedures to get a Cargo Data Interchange System (CARDIS) off the ground.

Eventually, it may prove possible to develop a wholly electronic system for the transfer of trade data, but there are many problems, both legal and technical. The bill of lading is a signed document issued at the port of shipment. It is thus acceptable proof of shipment on board the issuing carrier's vessel. By contrast, EDP involves a paperless transmission of data which lacks the kind of signature to which courts are accustomed. It is true that there may well be a documentary print-out both at the port of shipment and at the port of destination but the crucial stage of transmission of the data is not in documentary form and is not authenticated by a conventional signature. Where a contract or Convention prescribes the issue of a signed document, the court may have to consider whether electronically recorded data constitute a document and whether an electronic key designed to authenticate a message suffices as a "signature." Where a print-out at the port of destination is relied on, will this be acceptable as an original document or will objection be taken on the ground that it is not the same document as that produced at the port of shipment? What evidence will a court require in order to be satisfied that the information printed out at the port of destination corresponds to that which was fed in at the port of shipment?

A further problem arises where it is desired to deal with the goods in transit, *e.g.* by way of pledge to a bank or resale to a sub-buyer. A key feature of a bill of lading is that as a document of title it represents the goods, so that negotiation of the document transfers constructive possession.[57] The concept of negotiability, which depends on physical delivery of a document, cannot be replicated in a paperless system, and it would be necessary to adopt other legal devices. For example, the carrier could undertake in the contract of carriage to hold the goods to the order of each transferee notified to him by a duly authenticated communication, so that each such notification would bring about the desired transfer of constructive possession.[58]

At the technical level, the problems are even more formidable. First, the systems have to be developed. Next, they have as far as possible to be unified or made compatible. This is hard enough within a defined institutional framework such as that established by the banking community; it is ten times more difficult in the case of the diffuse organisations involved in the exportation of goods. Thirdly, the safety and security of the systems must as far as possible

[57] Assuming that these are identified. See above, p. 00.
[58] See Bergsten and Goode, *loc. cit.*, n. 55 above, p. 145.

be guaranteed. The elimination of documents removes one form of fraud but opens up the possibility of fraud and abuse in a different form, through illegitimate interference with computer systems. But that is another subject!

V

Reservation of Title and Tracing Rights in Goods, Products and Proceeds

1. INTRODUCTION

The Romalpa decision

More than a decade has now elapsed since Mr. Justice Mocatta delivered judgment in the famous *Romalpa* case,[1] a decision upheld by the Court of Appeal the following year in a controversial ruling that was to have a greater impact on commercial law than almost any other case decided this century. What *Romalpa* did was to establish that a seller who supplies goods under reservation of title and authorises his buyer to resell them on condition that he accounts for the proceeds of sale has an equitable right to trace those proceeds and to recover them from the buyer in a proprietary claim, so that the proceeds are not part of the buyer's assets and accordingly do not fall within the scope of a floating charge given by the buyer.

Though the equitable right to trace from property into proceeds is of long standing, and was recognized at least a century ago as available whether the disposition producing the proceeds was authorised or unauthorised,[2] almost all cases prior to *Romalpa* involved a tracing claim to proceeds of an unauthorised disposition. It therefore came as a distinct surprise to most lawyers to learn from *Romalpa* that tracing in equity was permitted even where the proceeds resulted from authorised resales made by the buyer as part and parcel of an ongoing business relationship with his seller.

It is doubtful whether the full implications of *Romalpa* were appreciated by the court at the time of the decision; indeed, even now they have not been fully worked out. What is clear is that the concept of an equitable proprietary right created by contract for the purpose of securing payment but not registrable as a security interest and therefore invisible to other parties dealing with the buyer has troubled the courts considerably in later cases, and every effort has

[1] [1976] 1 Lloyd's Rep. 443. The literature on this case is now substantial. For an up to date treatment, see Sally Jones "Retention of Title Clauses 10 years from Romalpa" (1987) 7 Co. Law 233; and Iwan Davies, [1984] 1 L.M.C.L.Q. 49; (1985) 129 S.J. 3, 26; [1985] 1 L.M.C.L.Q. 15.

[2] *Re Hallett's Estate* (1880) 13 Ch.D. 696.

been made to confine the efficacy of the so-called *Romalpa* clause as narrowly as possible.

In this final lecture, I propose to discuss the present state of the law in relation to the right of a title-reserving seller to follow, first, the goods themselves, secondly, new products resulting from their commingling with other goods and thirdly the proceeds of disposition of the goods. I shall begin by considering the effect of unauthorised conduct by the buyer and then go on to analyse the different forms of title reservation clause under which commingling and resale are authorised and the circumstances in which a purported reservation of title may be held to create a charge. I shall then examine the implications of the case law for the drafting of reservation of title clauses in sale contracts. In conclusion, I shall look at the impact of administration petitions and orders on the enforcement of reservation of title clauses under the Insolvency Act 1986, before ending with a general note on law reform. The *dramatis personae* in this presentation are as follows:

S = seller who reserves title
B = buyer who buys goods under reservation of title and later disposes of them in exchange for proceeds or makes them up into a new product
T1 = the person to whom B disposes of the goods and from whom he receives the proceeds in exchange
T2 = the person to whom B transfers the proceeds
TP = third party whose goods B commingles with those supplied by S.

The starting point: a reservation of title by S

The discussion which follows presupposes that S has in fact reserved title to the goods supplied to B. This is a question of construction of the contract. Without such a reservation, express or implied, there is no proprietary base from which S can claim an interest in the product. This point is sometimes overlooked and the assumption made that because the product resulted from S's materials S acquires a proprietary interest in the product. But if the property in the materials passed to B there is no basis upon which S can claim ownership of the finished product in the absence of an agreement for transfer to him of the property in the product and the performance of that agreement by an unconditional act of appropriation.

Suppose, for example, that S delivers to B a quantity of gold to be made up into gold bars. The parties may agree that the gold is to be transferred to B and the resulting bars sold back to S, in which case the property in the bars will not pass to S until there has been an unconditional act of appropriation by one party with the assent of the other.[3] But what if the contract contains neither a reservation of title clause nor a provision for sale back to S? Where the agreement is that S's gold will be worked on exclusively for his benefit and will thus come back to him, albeit in altered form, B can properly be treated as a bailee of the gold,[4] so that there is an implied reservation of title to this and the resulting gold bars will belong to S. The position is otherwise if the terms of the agreement are such that B is free to apply the gold for his own purposes—*e.g.* by sale or making up into bars or other products for third parties—and to supply to S bars made from gold belonging to B's general stock or obtained from others, so long as this is of equivalent description and quality. In such a case B is not a bailee of the gold received from S, for he is under no duty to return it to S even in altered form,[5] and in consequence S has no proprietary base from which to assert a claim either to what he supplied or to any bars not unconditionally appropriated to him.[6]

The position is not altered by the fact that several people supply gold to be made up into bars; for if none of them reserves title to what he supplies, whether expressly or by implication, there is no proprietary link between his input and the bars made by B and thus no basis either for individual claims to ownership by particular suppliers or for a co-ownership claim by all of them collectively.[7] Accordingly where the various contributors of gold impose no requirement that the ingots which B undertakes to make for them are to come, wholly or in part, from the gold they have supplied, so that B is free to use that gold for his own purposes and to fulfil his contracts with the contributors by utilising his existing stocks or gold obtained from other parties, ownership of the gold passes to B and a contributor obtains no proprietary interest in the commingled gold or in any ingot produced from it until that ingot has been

[3] See above, p. 19.

[4] This form of bailment was known in Roman law as *locatio operis faciendi*. See generally N. E. Palmer, *Bailment*, pp. 97–99, 501–507.

[5] As Professor Palmer puts it (*Bailment*, p. 97): "What is necessary [for a bailment] is that the goods themselves, whether in altered or in original form, should be returnable, and not merely some other goods of equivalent character or value. There must be a clear physical heredity between what has been delivered to the bailee and what must be returned."

[6] *South Australian Insurance Co. Ltd.* v. *Randell* (1869) L.R. 3 C.P. 101; *Chapman Bros.* v. *Verco Bros. & Co. Ltd.* (1933) 49 C.L.R. 306. See also *Clough Mill Ltd.* v. *Martin* [1984] 3 All E.R. 982, *per* Goff L.J. at p. 989: "Now it is no doubt true that, where A's material is lawfully used by B to create new goods, whether or not B incorporates other material of his own, the property in the new goods will generally vest in B, at least where the goods are not reducible to the original materials (see 2 Bl.Com. (14th ed.) 404–405)."

[7] See to the same effect Peter Birks, *An Introduction to the Law of Restitution*, pp. 378–380.

unconditionally appropriated to his contract.[8] Prior to that time he has a mere personal claim against B for manufacture and delivery of ingots of the agreed number, weight and description.

But where the agreement between a supplier and B is that the ingots are to come from the bulk of gold resulting from the commingling of B's input with that of B himself or of other suppliers, the court will be ready to infer an intention by each supplier to reserve title to the gold he has himself supplied prior to the commingling and an agreement that prior to the manufacture and appropriation of the gold bars each supplier is to have a proportionate interest in the commingled gold and the ensuing unappropriated gold bars. An instructive example is to be found in the recent decision of the Court of Appeal of New Zealand in *Coleman* v. *Harvey*.[9] In that case:

H came to an arrangement with C by which, in consideration of H continuing to supply C's company with material containing silver, H would deliver to the company a quantity of silver coins weighing about 330kg for refining and from the mass produced by commingling the melted down coins and the company's other source materials 166kg of fine silver (representing the quantity of silver estimated to be yielded by the coins H had supplied) would be extracted and made into ingots which would be stored for H until he required them. The coins and other materials were melted down and ingots produced but instead of setting these aside for H the company sold them to third parties. H did succeed in obtaining delivery of 49kg of silver, after which the company went into receivership. H sued C as a joint tortfeasor in converting the balance of H's silver.

At first instance H succeeded on the ground that C had acknowledged that the company was holding the silver on H's behalf, thus making it a bailee by attornment. On appeal, the Court of Appeal of New Zealand held that the conversion had already occurred before the act of attornment relied on, so that this could not found an action for conversion. However, the facts found by the trial judge showed that the company was not free to use the coins and the silver from them as it chose, with a mere duty to return the equivalent, but was required to supply to H ingots made from the silver extracted from the coins he had supplied and other source materials of the company itself. It was clear that neither H nor the company intended to give up ownership of what each had contributed to that mass. Accordingly until appropriation of ingots to the contract H and the company were co-owners of the mass, and of any resulting ingots, in the proportions of their respective contributions. Had the requisite number of ingots been set aside for H the company would thereby have relinquished its interest in such of its materials as went into those ingots,

[8] *South Australian Insurance Co. Ltd.* v. *Randell*, above.
[9] Unreported, 22 March 1989.

whilst H would have relinquished his rights to any remaining part of the mass incorporating the coins he had supplied. The contract was not one of mutuum or sale but a contract sui generis involving intermixture upon terms of co-ownership. C had participated in the company's disposition of the ingots to third parties whose identities were unknown, thereby depriving H of his right to possession, and this constituted a conversion by the company against H as its co-owner and also by C, who was accordingly liable in damages for the value of the ingots after deducting the value of the silver he had recovered.

2. *UNAUTHORISED CONDUCT BY THE BUYER*

(1) Following the Goods in their Original Form

Nemo dat quod non habet

Where S delivers goods to B under a contract of sale reserving title until payment and B disposes of them to T1 without S's authority, the starting position is that S can recover them from T1. S's interest is not a security interest but the retention of absolute ownership.[10] The well-known common law maxim that *nemo dat quod non habet* is now embodied in the Sale of Goods Act, s.21(1).

There are, however, five principal exceptions to this rule. T1 will acquire a good title from B if the latter sells with S's apparent authority[11]; if the goods are sold in market overt[12]; if the conditions of the Factors Act 1889, s.9, or the Sale of Goods Act, s.25, are satisfied (these sections do not apply if the conditional sale agreement is regulated by the Consumer Credit Act 1974[13]); if B, being in possession of the goods in his capacity as a mercantile agent with the consent of the owner, disposes of the goods as a mercantile agent[14]; or, finally, if the goods comprise a motor vehicle and T1 is either a bona fide private purchaser buying directly from B or the first private purchaser who buys from a trade or finance purchaser to whom B has disposed of the goods.[15] These exceptions to the *nemo dat* rule are fully discussed in the commercial law textbooks and I shall not discuss them further except to illustrate a few specific situations.

[10] See below, p. 95.
[11] This common law rule is expressly preserved by the Sale of Goods Act 1979, s.21(1).
[12] *Ibid.* s.22.
[13] Factors Act 1889, s.9, as amended by Consumer Credit Act 1974, Schedule 4, para. 2; Sale of Goods Act, s.25(2).
[14] Factors Act, s.2.
[15] Hire-Purchase Act 1964, ss.27–30.

Extinction of S's title where goods lose their identity

B's unlawful disposition is not the only event that may divest S of his exclusive title. This may also occur as the result of the goods losing their identity. Leaving aside the case of simple physical destruction, there are four situations in which loss of identity may occur as the result of B's actions, namely, where the goods have become incorporated into a building or annexed as a fixture, attached as an accession to other goods, mixed with other goods while preserving their physical characteristics and commingled with other goods so as to lose their physical identity and form an entirely new product.

(1) *Incorporation into a building or annexation as a fixture*

If B incorporates materials into a building they cease to be chattels. Similarly, if he annexes goods to land or buildings in such a way that they cannot be severed without material damage to the goods or to the land or buildings, the goods lose their identity as chattels and become fixtures forming part of the property and pass into the ownership of the landowner, subject to rights of severance. Typical cases are plant and machinery embedded in a building and building materials incorporated into the building in the process of construction. Where the sale agreement empowers S to enter upon the land and sever the *quondam* goods, this right is exercisable not only against B himself but also against B's lessor or mortgagee to the extent to which B himself has a right to remove the fixtures. The law on this subject is in fact considerably more complex than the preceding statement would suggest and I cannot explore it here. Reference should be made to the standard texts.[16]

(2) *Affixation as an accession*

S's goods may also lose their identity through becoming annexed to other goods as an accession, whereupon title passes to the owner of the principal goods. In deciding whether the degree of annexation results in S's goods becoming an accession, the test is similar to that

[16] Adkin & Bowen, *The Law Relating to Fixtures* (3rd ed.); Woodfall, *Landlord and Tenant*, paras. 1–1545 *et seq*. For a detailed treatment of the effect of affixation of goods held on hire-purchase, see R. M. Goode, *Hire-Purchase Law and Practice* (2nd ed.), Chap. 32; Guest & Lever, "Hire-Purchase Equipment Leases and Fixtures' (1963) 27 Conv.(N.S.) 30. See also O. P. Wylie, "Reservation of Ownership: A Means of Protection for Unsecured Creditors of Bankrupt Builders," (1978) 42 Conv.(N.S.) 37.

adopted for fixtures, *viz.* whether the goods are capable of removal from the principal goods without material damage to either.[17]

In the converse case where B annexes his own goods as an accession to S's goods, S can claim title to the whole under the above principle. However, S may also achieve this result by express stipulation in the contract. Thus it is common for hire-purchase and conditional sale agreements to provide that for the purpose of the agreement "the goods" are to include all additions and accessions. In such a case, title to the annexed goods passes by virtue of the contract and it is unnecessary to consider the question of accession. It follows that title to the accessory passes to S even where the degree of annexation is not such as would satisfy the common law test for an accession. A good illustration is the well-known decision of the High Court of Australia in *Akron Tyre Co. Pty. Ltd.* v. *Kittson.*[18] The plaintiffs let a vehicle on hire-purchase under an agreement which provided that "Any accessories or goods supplied with or for or attached to or repairs executed to the goods shall become part of the goods." The hirer fitted some tyres to the vehicle but subsequently removed the tyres and sold them to the defendant, who declined to deliver them up to the plaintiffs. The plaintiffs then sued the defendant in conversion.

It was held that:

(a) by virtue of the express provision in the hire-purchase agreement, ownership of the tyres passed to the plaintiffs when these were fitted by the hirer, so that it was unnecessary to consider the question of accession; and
(b) the hire-purchase agreement did not constitute a bill of sale of the tyres since the document did not of its own force pass the property in them. That did not come about until the occurrence of an external act, namely the placing of the tyres on the vehicle.

(3) *Commingling without loss of physical identity*[19]

Where B commingles S's goods with his own in such a way that, though the physical characteristics of the commingled goods are not changed, it is impossible to distinguish S's goods from those belonging to B, then if the commingling was authorised by S or effected in good faith the two parties become tenants in common of the mass in

[17] *Rendell* v. *Associated Finance Pty. Ltd.* [1957] V.R. 604; *Thomas* v. *Robinson* [1977] 1 N.Z.L.R. 385. See generally Goode, *op. cit.*, Chap. 33; A. G. Guest, "Accession and Confusion in the Law of Hire-Purchase" (1964) 27 M.L.R. 505.

[18] (1951) 82 C.L.R. 471.

[19] See Goode, *op. cit.* Chap. 33; Guest, *loc. cit.* n. 9, *supra*; Paul Matthews, "Proprietary Claims at Common Law for Mixed and Improvement Goods (1981) *Current Legal Problems* 159; R. A. Pearce, "A Tracing Paper," (1976) 40 Conv.(N.S.) 277 at pp. 282, 285.

proportion to their respective contributions, whereas if B acted with intentional wrongdoing the old rule was considered to be that S could claim the whole.[20] However, it is clear that in any proceedings by S the court has a wide discretion at common law[21] and by statute[22] to impose conditions on making an order in favour of S for specific delivery and may also take into account the value added by B in assessing damages for conversion. So unless the court thought the situation called for Draconian penalties it could, in making an order for specific delivery, impose a condition that S make B an allowance for the value added by B, and in awarding damages for conversion it could limit these to the value of S's goods prior to the commingling.

Examples of this form of commingling are the mixing of S's parcel of grain or sugar with B's, the commingling in a pipeline of oil or gas which previously was in separate streams belonging to S and B respectively, the storing of S's wine bottles with those of B where they are of the same description and have not been kept separately identifiable.[23]

Where the commingled goods are of substantially the same nature and quality, justice can usually be done to S by an order that he shall receive out of the mixture a quantity equal to what he put in, any loss through wastage or deterioration being borne by B and any doubt as to the quantity S put into the mixture being resolved in S's favour.[24]

It is necessary to distinguish the case where S starts with identified goods in his ownership which later become commingled with B's from those where one of the parties never acquires an interest in an identified article or bulk at all. In the former case, the bulk may be held in common; in the latter, as we have seen, there is a mere contract right.[25]

S's right to claim co-ownership of a pool of mixed assets does, of course, depend on his being able to show that what he contributed is still in the pool. This may not be easy where there is a continuous outflow of goods from B's premises to meet subsale contracts, so that S has to show it is his goods, not those of other contributors, that are left in the pool.

[20] *Spence* v. *Union Marine Insurance Ltd.* (1868) L.R. 3 C.P. 427; *Sandeman & Sons* v. *Tyzack & Branfoot Steamship Co. Ltd.* [1913] A.C. 680; *Gill & Duffus (Liverpool) Ltd.* v. *Scruttons Ltd.* [1953] 2 All E.R. 977; and *cf. Buckley* v. *Gross* (1863) 3 B. & S. 566.

[21] *Greenwood* v. *Bennett* [1973] 1 Q.B. 195.

[22] Torts (Interference with Goods) Act 1977, s.3(6).

[23] See above, pp. 22 *et seq.* and p. 35.

[24] *Indian Oil Corp. Ltd.* v. *Greenstone Shipping SA, The Ypatianna* [1987] 2 Lloyd's Rep. 286.

[25] See above, pp. 21, 71.

(4) *Processing causing loss of identity*

Where S's goods are not merely commingled but processed with the goods of B or TP in such a way that their physical identity is lost, so that they become converted into a different product, the same rule is applied as for commingling, so that subject to possible forfeiture of B's interest where he acted with intentional wrongdoing in processing S's goods the parties become tenants in common of the new product in the proportions of their respective contributions.[26] It is important to distinguish this case from the case where S purports to reserve title to the whole product, thereby creating a disguised form of charge. I shall return to this point later.

Where there is no commingling, and B simply applies his labour to convert S's materials into a different product (*e.g.* by converting grapes into wine, olives into oil) it seems that a different rule prevails, and that B, if acting innocently, becomes the owner of the product, albeit with a duty to compensate S for the value of his materials.[27] It would seem that this also applies where materials belonging to different owners are incorporated into a building. There is no right either at law or in equity to trace the materials into the building or its proceeds.[28]

(3) FOLLOWING THE PROCEEDS

Tracing proceeds of an unauthorized disposition at law and in equity

Let us assume that B wrongfully sells S's goods to T1 for £6,000, of which £1,000 is paid in cash as a down-payment, £2,000 is covered by an allowance for goods tendered by T1 in part-exchange and the balance of £3,000 is payable in six months' time. So the proceeds of S's goods are represented partly by money, partly by goods and partly by an account receivable. In whom do these proceeds vest at law and in equity?

The extent to which the common law recognized a right to trace from an article into its proceeds, and the legal characterisation of that right, is a matter of controversy.[29] As regards tangible proceeds,

[26] *Farnsworth* v. *Federal Commissioner of Taxation* (1949) 78 C.L.R. 504, *per* Latham C.J., at p. 510.

[27] *International Banking Corp.* v. *Ferguson Shaw & Sons*, 1910 S.C. 182. *cf.* J. C. L. Wickham, "The Struggle for Title," (1960–62) University of W.A.L.R. 472, at pp. 494 *et seq.*

[28] See below, p. 103, and Wylie, *loc. cit.*, n. 16, *supra*. Since all other materials suppliers are in the same boat, B's trustee may be able to scoop the pool.

[29] See R. A. Pearce, *loc. cit.*, n. 19, *supra*; Goode, "The Right to Trace and Its Impact in Commercial Transactions," (1976) 92 L.Q.R. 360, 528; Khurshid & Matthews, "Tracing Confusion," (1979) 95 L.Q.R. 78; Keeton and Sheridan, *Equity* (3rd ed.), Chapter XIX and literature there cited.

a number of writers seem to have assumed that the common law right to trace is proprietary in character and that *legal* title to tangible proceeds vests in S as the legal owner of the goods which produced the proceeds. Some thirteen years ago I argued that this "exchange-product" theory was untenable,[30] since it is axiomatic in the common law that title can pass only to the person intended by the transferor.[31] This, indeed, is why the common law steadfastly refused to recognise the trust, and why equity had to intervene to ensure that a party having a better right to the asset than the actual transferee was protected by requiring the transferee to hold the asset on trust for him. It is clear that in equity B, having received goods and money as the result of a wrongful disposition of S's asset, holds the proceeds on trust for S. Such a trust would be both unnecessary and impossible if *legal title* were to vest directly in S, for he would then be both legal and beneficial ownership and there would be no scope for the existence of a separate equitable interest under a trust.[32]

It follows that the common law right to trace is not proprietary but personal in character, and that S has the option of seeking a personal order for delivery up to him of the tangible proceeds or of adopting the unauthorised sale and suing in quasi-contract for money had and received by B, represented by the price paid to B by T1. It is agreed that what the courts of common law could not do was to order the transfer to S of the receivable vested in B, since their powers were limited to orders for the delivery up of possession or the payment of owner. To reach intangible proceeds, it is necessary for S to invoke the assistance of equity, which can impose a trust in relation to these as it can in relation to tangible assets.

S's common law personal right to trace tangible proceeds in the hands of B carries over to B's transferee, T2, except where he acquires title as a bona fide purchaser of the legal or equitable interest without notice.[33]

Whether it was possible at common law to trace money into a mixed fund is again a matter of controversy. The orthodox view is that it was not; my own, argued elsewhere,[34] is that the mixing of money was not an obstacle to a common law tracing claim, and that indeed just such a remedy was given in *Banque Belge Pour l'Etranger* v. *Hambrouck*.[35] Others have challenged the correctness of that

[30] (1976) 92 L.Q.R. 360 at pp. 366 and 367, n. 27, a conclusion supported by Khurshid & Matthews, above, at pp. 78 *et seq.*
[31] See above, p. 49.
[32] See below, pp. 101–102.
[33] See Goode, *loc. cit.* n. 29, above, at pp. 396–397.
[34] *Loc. cit.* at pp. 393–396.
[35] [1921] 1 K.B. 321.

decision,[36] though its authority does not appear to have been questioned in any subsequent case.

Be that as it may, since the proceeds of B's unauthorised disposition are treated in equity as held on a constructive trust for S,[37] it is hardly surprising that the equitable tracing right is that which is generally relied on, since it has the great advantage that it is proprietary in nature, so that it can be asserted not only against B himself but against his trustee in bankruptcy. This has the incidental effect of preserving S's personal remedies at common law, including the right to sue B's trustee in conversion if he fails to hand over goods received by B as proceeds of his unauthorised disposition.[38]

3. AUTHORISED DISPOSITIONS BY THE BUYER

I now turn to examine the effect of specific types of reservation of title clause under which the buyer is authorised to make the goods up into products and/or to resell them; and I shall discuss the circumstances in which a purported reservation of title may be considered a registrable charge.

Forms of title retention

Reservation of title can take a number of different forms. The so-called "simple" reservation of title clause is that which does no more than reserve title to particular goods until payment of the price of those goods. This type of clause remains common in the traditional form of conditional sale agreement used by finance houses. But encouraged by *Romalpa*, sellers have developed more extended clauses which are sometimes extremely elaborate. Such extensions take various forms which divide into two main types: those which are expressed to reserve title not only to the original goods but to their products and proceeds; and those which seek to secure not only the price of the particular goods to which they relate but other indebtedness of B to S, existing or future. Frequently the two forms of extension are combined, so that S seeks to retain title to the goods, their products and proceeds (including proceeds of proceeds) to secure the price of all goods from time to time supplied by S to B and (in the most expansive type of *Romalpa* clause) all other obligations of B to S. Finally, we have a case in which S transferred legal title but purported to reserve equitable ownership.[39] This is a drafting curiosity which I have never seen before or since, and which I shall briefly refer to a little later.

[36] Khurshid & Matthews, *loc. cit.* at pp. 91–93.
[37] *Taylor* v. *Plumer* (1815) 3 M. & S. 562; *Re Hallett's Estate* (1880) 13 Ch.D. 696.
[38] For an early example of equity coming to the aid of the law in this way, see *Taylor* v. *Plumer*, above.
[39] *Re Bond Worth Ltd.* [1980] Ch. 228.

Simple reservation of title is not a security interest

It has long been established that a seller who reserves title until payment does not on that account alone hold a security interest in law, even if (as is almost invariably the case) he retains title in order to secure the price. As pointed out by the Crowther Committee many years ago, English law has always drawn a sharp distinction between sale credit and loan credit and between title reservation and a purchase-money chattel mortgage. Security in the legal sense involves the grant by the debtor to his creditor of rights in an asset which the debtor himself owns or in which he has an interest. Reservation of title, by contrast, represents no more than an agreement between seller and buyer as to the conditions on which property is to pass. As we have seen, until such conditions are satisfied the buyer has a mere contract right, not an interest in the goods, so that in entering into the agreement he gives no rights over his own asset, merely a right to the seller to reserve title and to repossess his own property in the event of default. This was settled long ago in *McEntire* v. *Crossley Bros. Ltd.*[40] and has remained the law ever since, despite the recommendation of the Crowther Committee that the law should be changed to equate title reservation with a purchase-money security interest.[41]

Since a substantial amount of business is written by finance houses under hire-purchase and conditional sale agreements on the assumption that these do not create charges or any other form of security, it was with considerable consternation that financiers and their legal advisers awoke one morning to read of the judgment at first instance in *Clough Mill Ltd.* v. *Martin*,[42] in which a reservation of title clause was struck down as an unregistered charge, on the ground that since the clause covered not only the original goods but products as well, this converted it into a charge even as regards goods that had not been made up and were held by the buyer in their original state. Fortunately for the peace of mind of the credit industry, the judgment was reversed on appeal,[43] in a set of very interesting judgments to which I shall return in due course.

Enforcement of title reservation against third parties

In principle, as previously noted, the seller is entitled to assert his ownership not only against the buyer but against any third party into whose hands the goods come. But as we have seen, there are

[40] [1895] A.C. 457.
[41] *Report of the Committee on Consumer Credit* (Cmnd. 4596, 1971), Chap. 5.2.
[42] [1984] 1 All E.R. 721.
[43] [1984] 3 All E.R. 982.

many exceptions to the *nemo dat* rule. The seller will not be able to follow the goods into the hands of a third party where the buyer disposed of them with the seller's actual or ostensible authority or where one of the five principal statutory exceptions to the *nemo dat* rule applies.[44]

(2) Reservation of Title to Secure the Price—Seller Claims the Product

Tracing into a product

Frequently a seller supplies under reservation of title materials which are to be made up into products or alternatively are to be consumed in the process of manufacture. Examples thrown up by the cases include aluminium foil to be incorporated into other objects[45]; resin mixed with hardeners and wax emulsion to form a glue mix, which was then blended with wood chippings and pressed together to form chipboard[46]; synthetic fibre spun with other fibre into yarn which was then processed and woven into carpets[47]; diesel engines incorporated as a component of diesel generating sets[48]; and leather made up into handbags.[49]

In what circumstances is the seller, S, entitled to rely on his reservation of title clause to claim the product resulting from the commingling with his goods of goods belonging to the buyer, B, or a third party, TP?

(1) *Contract silent as to products*

Where the contract of sale makes no provision as to title to the products, S's position depends in most cases on whether the commingling constituted an intentional wrongdoing. If so, he can assert a legal title to the product[50] (as a tenant in common, if TP's goods were also incorporated), though as previously mentioned the court has a wide discretion as to the orders it can make to do justice between the parties. Where B's act of commingling was authorised or done in good faith, ownership of the product depends upon the construction of the contract. It may well be that the parties intended B to become sole owner, with a mere personal obligation to S to pay the price of the materials furnished by him. Alternatively (and this seems to be the presumption at common law) S and B (and TP, if

[44] See above, p. 88.
[45] *Aluminium Industrie Vaassen BV* v. *Romalpa Aluminium Ltd.* [1976] 1 Lloyd's Rep. 443.
[46] *Borden (U.K.) Ltd.* v. *Scottish Timber Products Ltd.* [1981] Ch. 25.
[47] *Re Bond Worth Ltd.* [1980] Ch. 228.
[48] *Hendy Lennox (Industrial Engines) Ltd.* v. *Grahame Puttick Ltd.* [1984] 2 All E.R. 152.
[49] *Re Peachdart Ltd.* [1984] Ch. 131.
[50] See above, p. 91.

any of his materials were used) become tenants in common of the product to the extent of their respective interests.[51]

Where, however, S's goods are not commingled with any goods of B or TP but are simply consumed in the process of manufacture, S has no claim to the product, in the absence of any contractual provision giving him an interest in the product. In such a case, S may, if the processing of his goods was done without his consent, sue for damages for conversion as an alternative to an action for the price; but if S consented to the processing, then his sole remedy is an action for the price. This point was well brought out in the decision of the Court of Appeal in *Borden (U.K.) Ltd.* v. *Scottish Timber Products Ltd.*[52] The sellers supplied resin on terms that the property in the goods sold was to remain in them until payment had been made for those goods and all others supplied up to the time of payment. It was known that the resin was to be made up into glue, which was to be incorporated with wood chippings into chipboard, so that in the ordinary way the resin would lose its physical identity in the process of manufacture within two days of its delivery. The contract contained no provision giving the sellers rights in the finished product.

It was held that no term could be implied extending the seller's title from the resin to the chipboard, and that their title to the resin ceased when this was consumed in the process of manufacture.

The court indicated that the position might well have been otherwise if the sellers' goods had not lost their physical identity but had simply become commingled with the buyer's goods.

> "Supposing I deposit a ton of my corn with a corn factor as bailee, who does not store it separately but mixes it with corn of his own. This, I apprehend, would leave unaffected my rights as bailor, including the right to trace. But a mixture of heterogeneous goods in a manufacturing process wherein the original goods lose their character and what emerges is a wholly new product is in my judgment something entirely different."[53]

(2) *Contract is expressed to give S sole title to the product*

Where S delivers materials to B to be made up into a finished product, and B is to provide no (or no significant) materials of his own but is simply to apply his labour to make the product, there seems no reason why the court should not give effect to a stipulation in the sale contract that until payment S is to remain the owner of the original goods before they are made up and the product after they have been made up. Moreover, since it is only S's materials that are

[51] The position is otherwise when S did not reserve title to the original goods. See above, p. 85.

[52] [1981] Ch. 25.

[53] *Ibid. per* Bridge L.J., at p. 41.

involved he is not seeking to reserve title to more than he originally supplied, so that it cannot be said that he is taking a charge or other security over an asset of B.

The position is apparently otherwise where the product comprises not only S's goods but materials supplied by B or TP. In that situation, *Clough Mill Ltd.* v. *Martin*[54] appears to establish that S's so-called retention of title will be construed as a charge to the extent that it purports to cover the whole product. It is evident that at least two members of the Court of Appeal were led to this conclusion with some reluctance. In the words of Oliver L.J.:

> " . . . I am not sure that I see any reason in principle why the original legal title in a newly manufactured article composed of materials belonging to A and B should not lie where A and B have agreed that it shall lie."[55]

What seems to have impelled the court to find that the agreement created a charge in so far as it purported to give S title to the product was that if its terms were construed literally as reserving absolute ownership to S, he would acquire a windfall as regards materials added by B, a result the court could not believe the parties intended; whilst if the product incorporated materials supplied by TP under a similar reservation of title provision one would have the prospect of two different sellers each claiming title under a *Romalpa* clause.

Where the circumstances show that after the commingling B is to be free to sell the product without keeping either the product or its proceeds separate from B's other property or money, it becomes impossible to say that he sells as S's fiduciary agent in the *Romalpa* sense, and a clause vesting title to the product in S will be construed as a charge. This was the ruling of Vinelott J. in *Re Peachdart Ltd.*[56]

(3) *Contract expressed to give S joint title to the product*

In the Irish case of *Kruppstahl AG* v. *Quitmann Products Ltd.*[57] Gannon J. carried this a stage further, holding that a provision by which S and B were to hold the product jointly in the ratio of the invoice value of S's goods to those of B's goods constituted a registrable charge, since S's interest was limited to the securing of B's indebtedness for the price of the goods supplied by S.

From the above decisions it would seem that if S were expressly to reserve an absolute sole interest, or an absolute joint interest, unrestricted by the amount of B's indebtedness, then though this might give him the windfall of B's labour and materials the agreement could not be struck down as an unregistered charge, since it

[54] [1984] 3 All E.R. 982.
[55] *Ibid.* at p. 993.
[56] [1984] Ch. 131.
[57] [1982] I.L.R.M. 551.

would not be limited in its effect to what was necessary to secure payment of the price. By qualifying his interest (either expressly or, as in the *Clough Mill* case, by what the court recognized as a strained construction of the contract, in order to avoid what was felt to be an unintended windfall for S) S makes it a security for the debt.

(3) Reservation of Title to Secure the Price—Seller Claims the Proceeds

Is there a duty to account?

Earlier, we looked at the case where B disposed of S's goods without S's authority.[58] In that situation, B will almost invariably be a constructive trustee of the proceeds, for since the sale of the original goods was wrongful B can hardly argue that he was entitled to treat the proceeds as his own.

The situation is entirely different where the sale by B is made with S's authority. In such a case, the question whether B is to be accountable to S for the proceeds as a constructive trustee or is simply to be S's debtor for the price of the goods bought by B depends on the construction of the contract. Where the contract prescribes an express duty to account for proceeds, the court is likely to regard this as imposing an obligation on B to hold the proceeds on trust for S.[59] If, however, the contract is silent, the court is likely to infer that B was not to be accountable for the proceeds but was merely to be a debtor to S, whose claim would thus be personal, not proprietary. A good illustration is provided by *Re Andrabell Ltd.*[60] The plaintiffs supplied travel bags to a company under contracts of sale reserving title until payment and allowing the buyer company 45 days' credit. The company resold the bags, paid the proceeds into its general bank account, thus commingling them with its other moneys, and then went into liquidation without having paid the price of the bags.

The plaintiffs' contention that they were entitled to trace the proceeds in equity into the bank account was rejected by Peter Gibson J. on the ground that, in contrast to the situation in *Romalpa*, there was no express acknowledgment of a fiduciary situation, no undertaking to keep the proceeds of sale separate or to account for them to

[58] See above, p. 92.

[59] *Aluminium Industrie Vaassen BV* v. *Romalpa Aluminium Ltd.* [1976] 1 Lloyd's Rep. 443. However, the position may be otherwise if, though the duty to account is imposed, S knowingly allows B to commingle the proceeds with his own moneys or otherwise treat them as his own, for B's right to do this is inconsistent with the existence of a fiduciary obligation as to the proceeds. See *Henry* v. *Hammond* [1913] 2 K.B. 515; *Re Bond Worth Ltd.* [1980] Ch. 228 at p. 261. Moreover, even where there is a trust, it is a separate question whether the trust is by way of charge or is merely declaratory of a right to the proceeds given to S from the outset under equitable rules of tracing. See below, p. 100.

[60] [1984] 3 All E.R. 407.

the plaintiffs and no contention (nor could it have been contended) that the company was selling as the plaintiffs' agent. Finally, the provision of 45 days' credit was hard to reconcile with the company's duty to account for the proceeds, which even on the plaintiffs' argument it would presumably have been entitled to retain for the period of the credit.

A similar conclusion had previously been reached by Staughton J. in *Hendy Lennox Ltd.* v. *Grahame Puttick Ltd.*[61] In both cases it was accepted that whilst on the facts the provision of credit was inconsistent with the existence of an equitable duty to account, this did not inevitably follow; indeed, in *Romalpa* itself the Court of Appeal, though accepting that the provision for credit was a formidable obstacle to the existence of a duty to account, held that the clear terms of the agreement—lacking in the latter cases—had to be given effect. This is plainly right. The sale agreement may, for example, be construed as providing that the buyer is to have 45 days' credit but subject to a duty to account for proceeds of sale on receipt, the transfer of such proceeds *pro tanto* reducing the buyer's price indebtedness. The duty to account thus cuts down the scope of the provision for credit but does not deprive it of effect, for the buyer remains entitled to avail himself of the full period of the credit except in so far as he receives proceeds of sale during that period.

Does the proceeds clause create a charge?

We have seen that where the contract contains an express provision requiring B to account for proceeds, this will usually be effective to make B a trustee of the proceeds for S instead of leaving S merely an unsecured creditor for the price. An entirely separate question is whether S's right to the proceeds is absolute or by way of consensual security. The distinction is of some importance because if the buyer is a company and the trust is by way of security it will usually be void if not registered as a charge on book debts.[62] The key question is whether, in making the resale which generated the proceeds, B acted on his own behalf or as S's bailee and fiduciary agent. If he acted on his own behalf, then it is *his* proceeds which he is undertaking to make over to S, and if the undertaking is limited to such part of the proceeds as is necessary to discharge B's indebtedness to S the court is likely to treat it as given by way of security.[63] Where, on the other hand, it is apparent from the construction of the contract that B held the goods as S's bailee and was disposing of them as his agent, then in undertaking to make over the proceeds B

[61] [1984] 2 All E.R. 152.
[62] Under ss.395 and 396 of the Companies Act 1985.
[63] *E. Pfeiffer Weinkellerei-Weineinkauf GmbH & Co.* v. *Arbuthnot Factors Ltd.* [1988] 1 W.L.R. 150; (1987) 3 B.C.C. 608.

is doing no more than agreeing to account for that which in equity belonged to S from the outset as the proceeds of his goods and to which he would anyway have had an equitable tracing claim.[64] Prima facie B is not a bailee and resells on his account.[65]

(4) Reservation of Title to Secure Other Indebtedness

Prior to *Clough Mill Ltd.* v. *Martin*[66] there had been some anxiety that a reservation of title clause expressed to secure not only the price of the particular goods sold but also other indebtedness of the buyer—*e.g.* for the price of all other goods supplied—might be held a disguised charge. Admittedly, such a clause was successfully invoked in the *Romalpa* case, but no argument was advanced on this point, nor was it discussed in the judgments. *Clough Mill* appears to lay these doubts to rest, though again it is not clear from the report of the case whether the point was fairly and squarely taken or how the arguments were deployed.

It is, indeed, hard to see why an all-moneys retention of title clause should change the character of the agreement, for it is, after all, open to the seller to impose any conditions he wishes for the transfer of ownership to his buyer. One can take the argument in stages. B orders goods from S, who refuses to accept the order until B has paid his account. Clearly S is entitled to do this. Now suppose that S agrees to accept the order but on terms that he will not deliver the goods until B has discharged his indebtedness. Plainly this is legitimate also and does not affect the character of the transaction as an ordinary contract of sale. Finally, B persuades S to let him have possession of the goods on terms that ownership is to pass only when B has settled his account in full. There seems no reason why this extra step should convert the reservation of title into a charge, for B is not conferring rights over his own goods. *Clough Mill* indicates, inferentially at least, that no charge is created.[67]

(5) Reservation of "Equitable and Beneficial Ownership"

Equitable ownership is the subject of grant, not reservation

A curious form of title reservation was invoked in *Re Bond Worth Ltd.*,[68] where S purported to transfer legal title but to reserve "equitable and beneficial ownership" to S. Since B was left entirely free to process the fibre supplied and to dispose of it and products made

[64] *Aluminium Industrie Vaassen B.V.* v. *Romalpa Aluminium Ltd.* [1976] 1 W.L.R. 676.
[65] *E. Pfeiffer Weinkellerei-Weineinkauf GmbH & Co.* v. *Arbuthnot Factors Ltd.*, above.
[66] [1984] 3 All E.R. 982.
[67] For a contrary view see William Goodhart, "*Clough Mill Ltd.* v. *Martin*—A Comeback For Romalpa?" (1986) 49 M.L.R. 96.
[68] [1980] Ch. 228.

with it in the ordinary course of business without constraint, it is not clear what the sellers thought they were achieving by this form of clause. In an admirable judgment, Slade J. (as he then was) pointed out that the legal and beneficial owner of an asset cannot "reserve" equitable ownership; all he can do is transfer the full legal title and take a grant back by way of equitable assignment, trust or charge. Since the so-called reservation was by way of security, the grant back was a charge; and as the chargor was left free to deal with the materials in the ordinary course of business the charge was a floating charge and should have been registered as such. This is clearly right. Where legal and beneficial ownership are combined there is no scope for equity to operate. The legal and beneficial owner does not have a legal title combined with an equitable title. He is simply the full owner.

4. *CONFLICTS BETWEEN THE SELLER AND THIRD PARTIES AS TO PROCEEDS*

Seller versus prior chargee of proceeds

Where S has reserved title in such a way as to have an equitable tracing claim to proceeds and B, prior to the contract of sale with S, has charged his book debts and other receivables to C and on B's sale of S's goods C lays claim to such proceeds as covered by his charge, who wins, C or S? There is no doubt that initially S's tracing claim has priority. C's charge over B's after-acquired receivables can only attach to receivables in which B has an interest for some moment of time. But if the receivables vest in S in equity from the moment of their birth, there is nothing to which C's charge can attach.

Can C jump ahead of S under the rule in *Dearle* v. *Hall* [69] by being the first to give notice to the debtors? Not if his charge is only a floating charge[70]; but the application of the rule in a contest between a fixed charge and an equitable tracing right remains a matter of controversy with which I have dealt elsewhere.[71]

Seller versus prior purchaser of proceeds

A similar unresolved priority problem arises where the conflict is between S as holder of an equitable tracing claim and a prior purchaser of the proceeds, *e.g.* a factoring company buying under a factoring agreement receivables arising from B's resales of goods acquired from S under reservation of title. The point potentially

69 (1828) 3 Russ. 1.
70 *Ward* v. *Royal Exchange Shipping Co. Ltd.* (1887) 58 L.T. 174; *Re Ind Coope & Co. Ltd.* [1911] 2 Ch. 223.
71 R. M. Goode, *Legal Problems of Credit and Security* (2nd ed.), pp. 120–121.

arose for decision in the *Arbuthnot Factors* case[72] but became moot in consequence of the finding that S's claim to the proceeds was as chargee, not as holder of an equitable tracing right.[73]

Seller versus subsequent chargee of proceeds

Similar considerations apply. S has provisional priority but if C takes a fixed charge without notice of S's tracing right and is the first to give notice to the debtors then arguably he displaces S under the rule in *Dearle* v. *Hall*.

Seller of building materials versus building owner

The supplier of building materials who reserves title until payment can in general assert his title against the building contractor or other buyer, and against the building owner, until such time as the materials have become affixed to or incorporated in the building. However, where the building contract provides for unfixed materials to vest in the building owner when he has paid an interim certificate and the certificate has been paid[74] which covers the value of the materials, then if they were supplied to the contractor under a contract of sale of goods the supplier may lose title under the Factors Act, s.9, and the Sale of Goods Act, s.25, on the basis that the contractor is a buyer in possession who has delivered them to the building owner as a bona fide purchaser for value and without notice of the supplier's rights. The position is otherwise where the contract between the main contractor and the supplier requires the latter to supply *and fix* the materials, for in that situation the materials are never intended to pass to the contractor as chattels and the contract is for work and materials, so that the above statutory provisions do not apply.[75]

5. *ESTABLISHING THE RESERVATION OF TITLE*

Essential requirements

In the wake of *Romalpa*, suppliers all over the country began to include reservation of title clauses in their contracts, stamp

[72] Above, n. 63.

[73] The learned judge held, correctly it is submitted, that as between a statutory and an equitable assignee priority remains governed by the rule in *Dearle* v. *Hall* and does not go to the statutory assignee despite his status as a legal purchaser for value without notice, for the effect of section 136 of the law of Property Act 1925 is that all assignees, statutory and equitable, take subject to equities.

[74] If it has not, the condition precedent to the vesting of the materials in the building owned is not satisfied, so that there is no sale or other disposition to him within the statutory provisions (*W. Hansom (Harrow) Ltd.* v. *Rapid Civil Engineering Ltd.* (1987) 38 B.L.R. 109).

[75] *Dawber Williamson Roofing Ltd.* v. *Humberside County Council* [1979] C.L.Y. 212.

"Romalpa" on their invoices and assert proprietary claims to the goods on the buyer's bankruptcy. Initially, many of these claims were accepted, but over time receivers and liquidators became much more hard-headed, demanding clear evidence that the goods claimed were in fact the subject of a contractual provision for reservation of title. In consequence, a considerable number of these claims are now rejected.

In order for S to establish title to goods under a reservation of title clause three essential requirements must be met:

(1) The reservation of title must be a term of the contract.[76]
(2) The goods held by B or his trustee must be identifiable as those, or as including those, supplied by S under reservation of title.[77]
(3) The amount secured by the reservation of title must be wholly or partly unpaid.[78]

Making reservation of title a term of the agreement

It is necessary to S to show that his stipulation as to reservation of title was effectively incorporated as a term of the contract. The methods of showing this have been conveniently summarised by Boreham J. in *John Snow & Co. Ltd.* v. *DBG Woodcroft & Co. Ltd.*,[79] in which the plaintiffs successfully contended that their reservation of title clause had become a term of their various contracts with the defendants. Incorporation may be established by any of the following means:

(1) Embodiment of the term in a contract document signed by B.
(2) Embodiment of the term in an unsigned document which B was aware contained contract terms, even if he was not aware of their purport.
(3) Embodiment of the term in an unsigned document where S has done all that was reasonably sufficient to bring the terms to his notice. In this case, it is not necessary for S to show that B knew the document contained contractual provisions. What constitutes reasonable notice depends on the circumstances. Where a particular term relied on is very unusual, so that a party would have no reason to suspect its incorporation in the document, it may be necessary for the term to be drawn to his attention specifically. Reservation of title clauses are now so common that provided S has done what was necessary to bring the existence of the terms as a whole

[76] See below.
[77] See below.
[78] See below.
[79] (1984) May 25, unreported.

to B's notice, this suffices to give contractual effect to such a clause even if it was not specifically drawn to B's attention.

Ineffective incorporation

An alleged stipulation for reservation of title will not be effectively incorporated if the term is sought to be imposed after the making of the contract,[80] if it was in an unsigned document neither known to be contractual nor brought to B's notice or if it is excluded by countervailing terms effectively imposed by the buyer. This last case arises in the so-called "battle of the forms" where B places an order on stated terms, expressed to be overriding, and S purports to accept on different terms, including reservation of title. In such a case, S's purported acceptance is in reality a counter-offer, but if B proceeds with the transaction without objection he will usually be taken to have assented to the counter-offer by conduct.[81]

Many sellers whose contracts do not provide for reservation of title assume that the same effect can be achieved by stamping a reservation of title notice on their invoices. However, the dispatch of an invoice containing such a notice is ineffective as regards the contract to which it relates, for the contract has already been concluded and it is not open to the seller to vary the terms unilaterally. But if the seller consistently stamps his invoices with a reservation of title provision, and the buyer does not object, the seller may be able to argue that as regards *subsequent* contracts an agreement for reservation of title is to be implied from the course of dealing between the parties.

Identification of the goods as, or as including, S's goods

The onus is in general on S to show that the goods taken over by B's trustee are S's goods and not those of B or a third party. This may be difficult if B obtains goods of the same description from several suppliers, and if S is wise he will seek to identify his goods by a serial number or other identifying mark not readily removable. There is one case in which the onus shifts to the trustee. Where B has commingled S's goods with his own and the terms of the contract preclude him from disposing of S's goods, then the presumption against B's committing a breach of duty comes into play[82] and it will be assumed that B disposed of his own goods before selling those belonging to S.

[80] See *Olley* v. *Marlborough Court Ltd.* [1949] 1 K.B. 532, which held that a post-contract notice disclaiming liability for loss or theft of articles was held ineffective.
[81] *Butler Machine Tool Co. Ltd.* v. *Ex-Cell-O Corp. (England) Ltd.* [1979] 1 All E.R. 965.
[82] See above, p. 53.

Establishing that the sum secured by the title reservation is unpaid

Finally, S must show that B has failed to discharge the indebtedness secured by the reservation of title clause. Where the clause secures the whole of B's indebtedness all S needs to do is prove the unpaid balance, and it is not necessary for him to allocate B's payments as between one item of goods and another. Where the clause secures only the price of the particular goods supplied under the contract embodying the clause, and several such items have been supplied on the same terms, the matter is at first sight more difficult. Should B's payments be attributed to the different goods in the order of purchase, and if so on the basis of first in, first out (FIFO) or last in first out (LIFO)? Should the goods be treated as paid for in the order in which they are disposed of by B? Or should some other basis of allocation be adopted.

In fact, the problem is readily resolved by reference to well-established common law rules of appropriation. Where the dealings between S and B are reflected in a current account, then under the rule in *Clayton's Case*[83] the account is treated as a single blended fund and payments by B are set against the earliest indebtedness first. This presumption is rebuttable by proof of a contrary agreement, whether express or by conduct or course of dealing. In the absence of a current account, it is open to B, at the time he makes the payment, to appropriate it to a particular debt but if he fails to do so the right of appropriation passes to S, who is entitled to exercise it at any time before some act or event which would make it inequitable for him to exercise the right.[84] However, there is nothing to prevent S from reserving in the sale contract an express power to appropriate, notwithstanding any purported appropriation by B to the contrary, and this is obviously a sensible precaution.

6. *THE BUYER AS AGENT*

Several of the cases refer to B selling as S's agent. However, it is clear from the previously quoted dictum of Lord Roskill in the *Romalpa* case[85] that this "agency" is of the "commission" type, that is, internal to the relationship between S and B. As between B and his purchase, B resells as principal, and S is not a party, nor can he sue or be sued on the contract even as an undisclosed principal. It follows that only B is liable in contract for non-conformity of the goods with the contract and that, in the absence of an assignment of rights, only B can sue the sub-purchaser for the price.

[83] (1816) 1 Mer. 529.
[84] See *Chitty on Contracts* (25th ed.), Vol. 1, para. 1424 and cases there cited.
[85] See above, p. 84.

Let me now summarise the implications of all this for the draftsman of sale contracts who wishes as far as possible to safeguard S against the consequences of B's insolvency by reliance on a *Romalpa* clause.

Contents of the title reservation clause

The reservation of title clause should be so drafted as to emphasise S's proprietary rights and his interest in the goods, their products and proceeds. To that end, it is desirable to build in as many control provisions as are commercially feasible, always bearing in mind the importance of ensuring that the procedures laid down by the contract are in fact followed by the parties, so that the contractual provisions are not open to attack as disguising the true nature of the transaction. The reservation of title clause should provide that:

(1) B is to hold the goods as S's fiduciary agent and bailee;
(2) B, in so far as empowered to resell, sells as principal in relation to the sub-purchaser and has no right to commit S to any contractual relationship with or liability to any third party, but that as between S and B the latter is to sell as fiduciary agent;
(3) any resale by B is to be on commercially reasonable terms;
(4) B is to keep the goods separate from his own and those of third parties, properly stored, protected and insured;
(5) B is to account for all proceeds, tangible or intangible, including insurance proceeds and proceeds of proceeds;
(6) B is to keep all proceeds separate from his own and from those of third parties and is to keep all tangible proceeds properly stored, protected and insured;
(7) S is to have power to appropriate payments to such goods and accounts as he thinks fit, notwithstanding any purported appropriation by B to the contrary.

Separate clauses should provide for S's rights to products resulting from the application of labour to his goods, whether unmixed or commingled with materials of B or third parties. In the case of commingled parties, it is likely that such a clause will be held to constitute a registrable charge, since S is taking rights over materials not previously vested in him.

Clear incorporation

Finally—and this cannot be too strongly emphasised—ensure that the reservation of title clauses are clearly set out in the sale contract or incorporated into it by reference, and that the seller is made aware of the necessity of contracting by reference to the terms set out and does not fall into the trap of concluding a sale contract in general terms first and then seeking to impose reservation of title on the buyer after the contract has been made.

8. THE EFFECT OF ADMINISTRATION PETITIONS AND ORDERS ON THE ENFORCEMENT OF RESERVATION OF TITLE PROVISIONS

The Insolvency Act 1986, re-enacting the Insolvency Act 1985, contains provisions by which a company that is or is likely to become insolvent may be placed in administration for the purpose of securing its survival as a going concern, the approval of a voluntary arrangement, the sanctioning of a scheme under section 425 of the Companies Act 1985 or a more advantageous realisation of the company's assets than would be effected on a winding-up.[86]

The purpose of the statutory provisions is to give the company a breathing space in which to have its affairs put in order by the administrator appointed by the court; and this breathing space is procured by a statutory freeze on the enforcement of real and personal rights against the company pending the hearing of a petition for an administration order and during the currency of any order that is made.[87] This freeze extends to the repossession of goods held by the company under a hire-purchase agreement,[88] which for this purpose includes a conditional sale agreement, a chattel leasing agreement and a retention of title agreement.[89] A chattel leasing agreement is an agreement for the bailment of goods which is capable of subsisting for more than three months.[90] A retention of title agreement is defined in rather remarkable terms as an agreement for the sale of goods which does not constitute a charge on the goods but under which, if the seller is not paid and the company is wound up, the seller will have priority over all other creditors as respects the goods or any property representing the goods.[91] Since this would seem to encompass all conditional sale agreements as well as non-instalment sales wih reservation of title it is not clear

[86] Insolvency Act 1986, s.8.
[87] *Ibid.* ss.10(1), 11(3).
[88] *Ibid.* ss.10(1)(b), 11(3)(b).
[89] *Ibid.* s.10(4). "Conditional sale agreement" and "hire-purchase agreement" have the same meanings as in the Consumer Credit Act 1974 (*ibid.* s.436). By section 189(1) of the Consumer Credit Act "conditional sale agreement" means an agreement for the sale of goods or land under which the purchase price or part of it is payable by instalments, and the property in the goods or land is to remain in the seller (notwithstanding that the buyer is to be in possession of the goods or land) until such conditions as to the payment of instalments or otherwise as may be specified in the agreement are fulfilled."
[90] Insolvency Act 1986, s.251.
[91] *Ibid.*

what purpose is served by having conditional sale agreements as a distinct category.

The precise effect of the statutory provisions is unclear. So long as the sale agreement continues on foot the company presumably remains free to use the goods without being liable to be sued for the price, though in practice an administrator may pay at least the use value of the goods in order to prevent an application to the court by the seller on the ground of prejudice under section 27 of the Insolvency Act. However, there appears to be nothing to prevent the seller from terminating the agreement under powers contained in it (*e.g.* for default in payment) and though he cannot repossess the goods the termination would seem to be effective to deprive the company of its right to use the goods.

Where, on an application by the administrator, the court is satisfied that the disposal (with or without other assets) of any goods in the possession of the company under a hire-purchase agreement[92] would be likely to promote the purpose or one or more of the purposes specified in the administration order, the court may by order authorise the administrator to dispose of the goods as if all the rights of the owner under the agreement were vested in the company.[93] However, it must be a condition of such an order that:

(a) the net proceeds of the disposal, and
(b) where those proceeds are likely to be less than such amount as may be determined by the court to be the net amount which would be realised on a sale of the goods in the open market by a willing vendor, such sum as may be required to make good the deficiency,

are to be applied towards discharging the sums payable under the hire-purchase agreement.[94] The purpose of an order for sale is thus not to swell the assets of the company available for the general body of creditors but to facilitate the continuance of the company's business by allowing stock and other goods held on hire-purchase to be disposed of without the sale being blocked by those holding rights under reservation of title clauses.

9. THE REFORM OF THE LAW RELATING TO RESERVATION OF TITLE

The present law on reservation of title is profoundly unsatisfactory. Since the effect of the Sale of Goods Act is that the buyer does not acquire ownership (even beneficial ownership) until payment, the reservation of title does not constitute the grant of a security interest,

[92] As defined by the Act. See text and n. 88 above.
[93] Insolvency Act 1986, s.15(2).
[94] *Ibid.* s.15(5).

for the buyer is not giving security rights over his own goods, he is merely agreeing to the conditions on which ownership is to pass to him. It follows that if the seller repossesses the goods on the buyer's default and a resale produces a surplus above the balance of the price outstanding under the sale agreement the buyer has no legal interest in that surplus, which the seller (unlike a mortgagee) can retain for himself. It follows also that reservation of title is not registrable as a security interest, so that its existence is not visible to innocent third parties purchasing the goods from the buyer or to administrative receivers dealing with the goods in the belief that they are the property of the debtor company.

Some 18 years have elapsed since the Crowther Committee drew attention to these problems and recommended that United Kingdom law be changed along the lines of Article 9 of the American Uniform Commercial Code to treat sales under reservation of title as fully fledged purchase-money security interests, with the consequence that the buyer would be equated with a mortgagor and be given an equity of redemption and an interest in any surplus resulting from resale and the reservation of title would become registrable in the same way as a purchase-money chattel mortgage.[95] Those recommendations were supported by the Cork Committee on Insolvency Law and Practice[96] but have not yet been implemented. More recently the Department of Trade and Industry commissioned Professor Diamond to report on the reform of personal property security law.[97] Professor Diamond's Report has now been published.[98] This broadly follows the recommendations of the Crowther Committee (with modifications in the light of further examination and of North American experience) and proposes the adoption of a new personal property security law along the lines of Article 9 and the Canadian Personal Property Security Acts.

[95] *Report of the Committee on Consumer Credit* (Cmnd. 4596, 1971), paras. 4.2.2–4.2.5, Part V and Appendix III.

[96] *Report of the Review Committee* (Cmnd. 8558, 1982), Chap. 37.

[97] Professor Diamond's consultation paper "Security Interests in Property other than Land" (Consultation Paper SS4 AAN) was issued in 1986.

[98] *A Review of Security Interests in Personal Property* (HMSO, 1989).

Appendix

TRANSCRIPT OF THE JUDGMENT IN THE CASE OF THE LONDON WINE COMPANY (SHIPPERS) LTD

IN THE HIGH COURT OF JUSTICE
CHANCERY DIVISION

Royal Court of Justice,
Friday, 7th November, 1975.

Before:–
MR JUSTICE OLIVER

RE LONDON WINE COMPANY (SHIPPERS) LTD.
(Application of Receiver)

(Tape Transcription by Cherer & Co., 34 Essex Street, Strand, London, WC2R 3AT. Telephone Number: 01–583–4121)
MR. L. J. MORRIS SMITH (instructed by Messrs. Wilde, Sapte & Co., London) appeared for the Receiver (Applicant).
MR. R. A. K. WRIGHT, Q.C. and *MR. ROBIN POTTS* appeared for the Respondents R. Strong, L. Button, M. F. Bailey & S. Pilkington.
MR. S. STAMLER, Q.C. and *MR. F. REYNOLD* (instructed by Messrs. Denton, Hall & Burgin, London) appeared for the Respondents Vinum, Ltd. and Canadian American Bank, S.A.
MR. T. H. BINGHAM, Q.C. and *MR. J. F. MUMMERY* appeared for the Respondents The National Westminster Bank, Ltd.

JUDGMENT

(*As approved by Judge*)

The London Wine Company (Shippers) Ltd. (to which I will refer as "the Company") issued a debenture to the National Westminster Bank Ltd. It was in the Bank's usual form of all-moneys charge and, in addition to a fixed charge on certain specified assets, it created a floating charge on the assets of the Company. It provided that the Company should not without the written consent of the Bank create any charge in priority to or ranking *pari passu* with the floating charge.

On the 28th August 1974 (which has been referred to in these proceedings as "the relevant date") the Bank, under a power contained in the Debenture, appointed a Mr. Curtis to be the Receiver of the

Company's business and undertaking. No question arises as to the validity of the charge or as to the propriety or validity of the Receiver's appointment.

The summons before me is one issued by the Receiver under section 369 of the Companies Act 1948 for directions as to the disposition of certain stocks of wine which are claimed by the Bank (which is a Respondent to the summons) to be the property of the Company and thus subject to the Bank's charge.

The question arises in this way. The business of the Company at all material times has been that of dealers in wine and in the course of that business it has, from time to time, acquired substantial stocks of wine which have been deposited in various warehouses, either in bond or after payment of duty. Some of the wine has been bought by the Company on its own account but substantial quantities have been sold to customers buying either for laying down or as an investment. In a great many cases there has been no appropriation from bulk of any wine to answer particular contracts, and it is with this class of case that the questions raised by the present summons arise.

So far at any rate as concerns the types of transaction with which the present summons is concerned the modus operandi, as it emerges from the evidence before me, was as follows. Brochures were sent out explaining how customers could buy for investment. For present purposes the relevant brochure is that produced in August 1972 and entitled "Claret Investment. How it works and why." This explained the classification of clarets and the advantages to be derived from the expected capital appreciation and contained a brief description of how the purchase was to be effected from the Company's point of view. That was in these terms:— "The system operated by this company is as follows. We sell you the wine by the dozen LYING IN BOND or if it is an extremely recent vintage LYING IN BORDEAUX"—I pause to mention that none of the questions raised by the present summons relate to purchasers of wine of this last-mentioned description—. The circular continues: "You receive a certificate from us or for a small extra charge direct from the Bond establishing that you are the beneficial owner of the wine."

People interested in buying wine ordered it from the company by filling in an application form or by telephone, but the company also published investment price lists which set out the terms and conditions of purchase and the evidence of Mr. Baring, the Company's former Chairman and Managing Director, is that these are the terms and conditions which would have applied to the purchases by the first, second and fifth respondents, Mr. Strong, Mr. Button and Mrs. Pilkington. He produces the investment Price List for May 1974 which has, on the back page, a section headed "Terms and Conditions."

I will read these so far as they are material.

"1. Storage charges of 20p per case per quarter or part thereof are chargeable on goods stored by us, together with insurance at 75p per annum per £100 of the current market value.

"2. A Document of Title will be sent to you in respect of wines stored by us on your behalf as soon as payment has been made, together with a buy-back guarantee when applicable.

"3. The following charges must be added to the 'Lying in Bond' price if delivery is required." (There follows a specification of charges for duty, delivery, and documentation).

Clause 4 deals with V.A.T., and I need not, I think read it.

"5. All goods and the documents relating thereto shall be subject to a particular lien for all monies owing in respect of the goods and also to a general lien for all sums owing to the company either by customers or any person who has been the owner of the goods whilst in the possession of the company" . . . and there follows a power of sale.

So the contemplation clearly was that the wine would belong to the purchaser and would be stored for him by the Vendor. When an order was received from a customer, an invoice was prepared and sent to him. The invoices in the case of each class of purchaser represented in the instant case are in evidence. They are all, in all material respects, in the same form and I can take as typical that exhibited by the Receiver in the case of the first respondent, Mr. Strong. It is addressed to the customer, numbered and dated and the printed form contains a number of columns, one headed "Quantity and Description," one headed "Price per Dozen" and one headed "Value." Under the first there are typed at the top the words "Placed on paid reserve." This does not, as one might perhaps suppose, mean that the goods described in the Invoice had been segregated and put on one side for the customer. Mr. Baring's evidence is that this is an expression commonly used in the trade to signify that the wine is not to be delivered but is to be kept in warehouse. Although this is nowhere stated in terms, it seems that payment was expected and was in fact made on what Mr. Baring says are the usual terms in the trade, that is to say, within thirty days. Then, under the words "placed on paid reserve" there appears descriptions of the various wines comprised in the invoice, as for instance, "40 dozen Volnay Santenots 1969 Domaine Jacques Prieur D.B." This must, I think, mean Domaine Bottled. In the second column, in addition to the price per dozen, there is typed in a note of the type of sale for instance: "Duty paid delivered" or "Lying in bond." The former signifies, of course, that the wine concerned is out of bond and in this case there is an additional charge for V.A.T. The final column contains the total price payable. So much for the invoice.

When the customer paid for the wine invoiced to him in this way, the Company sent him the Certificate of Title referred to in the brochure and conditions, and it is not disputed by the Bank that the purpose of this was to enable the customer to establish his title to the wine sold if he wished to sell third parties or to raise money on it. That certificate took the form of a letter and again Mr. Strong's case may be taken as typical. The letter is on the Company's headed notepaper and reads: "We have sold to you the under-mentioned wines, which have been duly paid for, and this letter confirms that you are the sole and beneficial owner of these wines." There then follows a description of the wines and the relative invoice number, as for instance: "40 cases 12/1," this presumably means cases of 12 full size bottles, "Volnay Santenots 1969 Domaine Jacques Prieur D.B. (Inv. 10579)." In the case of the Respondent, Mr. Bailey, the letter is not in evidence, but I have no reason to doubt that it was sent out in accordance with the Company's normal procedure.

Now here so far as the Customer was concerned, the matter ended until he either wished to sell, to pledge his wine or part of it or to withdraw some or all of it for consumption. As indicated in the conditions to which I have referred—and it is Mr. Baring's evidence that this was the norm except where special arrangements were made—the Company, in addition to the purchase price, charged for storage and insurance.

Theoretically the customer should have received periodical invoices for these charges, but Mr. Baring's evidence is that the workload in the office never permitted this to be done in fact, but customers would certainly be invoiced for any charges not previously paid when they took delivery or sold their wine. The charges raised were not the actual cost to the Company of storage and insurance, but contained a profit element to cover the costs of office administration.

The Company issued from time to time leaflets tendering to customers news on the progress of the wine market and advice on whether to hold or to realise, but apart from these and (possibly) intermediate invoices for storage and insurance, the customer would hear no more until he sought in some way to deal with the wine that he had bought.

So, so far as the customer was concerned, he was the purchaser of a specified number of unidentified cases of wine of a particular vintage, described as "duty paid delivered" or "lying in bond" and although he might well think that, once he had paid the price the Company would operate some machinery for segregating and identifying certain specific cases as earmarked for his purchase, there was no representation, or certainly no express representation, that this had been or would be done, and in fact it was not.

What occurred so far as the Company was concerned was that it maintained a stock book and a customer's paid reserve book. When a sale took place an entry was made in the stock book. This would allocate the wine sold to a particular consignment reference number at a particular warehouse but there would be no notification of the sale to the warehouse concerned except in circumstances where the customer wanted to mortgage his wine, as, it appears, not infrequently happened. The customer's paid reserve book was in two cross-reference parts, one containing the names of the customers and the other the designation of the warehouse or warehouses to which the customer's purchase had been allocated in the stock book. What happened when the customer disposed of all or part of the wine purchased by him is illustrated by the correspondence exhibited by Mr. Baring. In such circumstances it appears to have been the practice of the Company to send to the customer-vendor a letter cancelling the previous letter of title to the appropriate extent. For instance, the Respondent, Mr. Bailey, bought 85 dozen cases of Ch. Margaux 1966 in 1971 and the usual letter of title was sent to him on the 17th January 1972. In April 1973 he sold 50 cases and a letter was sent to him in the following terms: "This letter cancels your title to the under-mentioned wine originally given to you in our letter of the 17th January 1972; —50 cases "Chateau Margaux (inv. 8778)." In May, he sold the balance of 35 cases and a similar letter was sent to him.

I have already mentioned that there was no notification of the sale to the warehouseman. Equally there was no notification to the Company's insurers and in the later stages the insurance was either under a special block policy effected by the Company or was effected by the warehouseman. If, in the course of the delivery of the wine when withdrawn by the customer, there was a breakage, then an appropriate credit would be made by the Company to the customer.

Where the customer wanted to mortgage his wine, the warehouseman was notified. The best documented ordinary example of such a transaction is that of the Respondent Mr. Bailey and this may, I think, be taken as typical. There are rather special circumstances in the case of the Respondent Vinum Ltd. and its mortgagees with which I shall have to deal a little later. What appears to have happened in the ordinary way was this: either the customer or the chargee would notify the Company that the customer had charged his wine. The Company would then write to the warehouseman, or warehousemen storing the consignment to which the customer's purchase had been allocated in the Company's stock book instructing him or them to hold the appropriate quantity of wine in the name of the chargee and either requesting the warehouseman or warehousemen to send to the chargee a form of letter confirming that this had been done or to furnish warehouse warrants for the wine. The confirmatory letter seems to have taken substantially the same form in each case: "We confirm that we are holding the undermentioned wines in the name of the ——— Bank (giving the address) and that they will not be released without the written authority of the Bank."

The Warehouse warrant or receipt was a document addressed either to the Company or to the Chargee and stating that the Warehouseman had stored "for your account" at such and such a warehouse so many cases of a particular wine. In some (but not all) of the receipts the description of the wine is preceded by the words "Ex London Wine Co. (Shippers) Ltd." When the customer wished any of the wine to be sold, it appears that he would instruct the Company to effect the sale and the chargee would then forward the warehouse receipts to the Company together with an authority to the warehouseman to release the wine against an undertaking by the Company to account for the proceeds of sale.

Again there never was, in general, (at any rate in the cases which I have to consider) any segregation or appropriation of the wine in the warehouse until delivery to the purchaser. Evidence has been filed by a Mr. Porter who was a director of a number of warehouse Companies with whom the Company has substantial dealings. He sets out the modus operandi, so far as his warehouses were concerned, in the case of wine held in bond for investment. The wine is shipped direct to warehouse by the importer (in this case the Company) and held to the importer's order, each consignment being given a reference number. This would be related to the Customs Bond number which is assigned to the consignment (commonly a container load) when the goods are landed and which applies to that particular consignment or parts of it so long as it lies in bond. A Stock control card is then opened under each reference number and upon it are entered particulars of sales or charges which have been notified to the warehouseman. Thus, in so far as transactions have been notified to the warehouseman (and Mr. Baring's evidence is that, in general, this would only be done when the wine was charged as security) the stock control card will bear a note that out of that particular consignment number so many cases (without identifying them) are held to the order of such and such a chargee or transferee. At the actual point of storage, there is attached to each consignment a bin card on which is noted any physical withdrawal of the wine, so that the storekeeper can know at a glance how many cases remain in each consignment. It is generally impracticable to segregate and identify particular cases of wine and allocate them to individual purchasers and no attempt is made to do so, so that the wine is stored in bulk and no segregation of individual parcels take place until actual delivery is made to the purchaser or transferees from him.

On the relevant date there were held in various warehouses to the order of the Company or of chargees or transferees of customers of the Company very large bulk stocks in respect of which there had been no appropriation of individual cases, and the questions raised in this case related to three (originally four) types of transaction.

The first, which is typified by Mr. Stone, is the case where a single purchaser of a particular wine by generic description has purchased what was in fact the Company's total stock of that wine at the date of the purchase but where there has been no subsequent appropriation and where, apart from the so-called certificate of title, there has been no acknowledgment by the company or the warehouseman that wine of that description is held to the purchaser's order. Thus in Mr. Strong's case, he purchased 36 dozen and 11 bottles of Vosne Romanee les Genevrieres 1969 which was all that the Company had of that particular wine. That quantity was and is lying at Messrs. Porter & Laker's warehouse and is identifiable, but it has not been marked or otherwise appropriated to Mr. Stone's contract and, so far as Porter & Laker are concerned, is held for the Company. The wine was included in an invoice which covered several other types of wine and these were also included in the Company's letter of confirmation. The reference to the odd 11 bottles makes it look at first sight as if this was a specific parcel—there were occasions when the Company offered small "bin-end" quantities under specific lot numbers—but Mr. Curtis' evidence is that there were other sales in this category which related to numbers of whole cases; he has no evidence that Mr. Strong's case was any different.

The second category of transaction which is typified by Mr. Button is similar to the first except that in this case there were a number of purchasers of wine of a particular description whose purchase together exhausted the whole of the Company's stocks of wine of that description, which stocks were and are held by a number of different warehousemen.

The third category, typified by Mr. Bailey is similar to category 2, save that the purchasers did not exhaust the Company's stocks and that in this case, although there was no act of appropriation, there was an acknowledgment given by the warehouseman to Mr. Bailey's mortgagee the National Westminster Bank acting through its Wantage branch, that the appropriate quantity of wine was held to its order.

In this category there are two additional respondents (numbered for convenience 3(a) and 3(b)) Vinum Ltd., and its mortgagees the Canadian American Bank S.A. In order to avoid confusion with the Respondents, the National Westminster Bank Ltd., I will refrain from calling the Respondent 3(b) "the Bank" and will call it by the name under which it originally carried on business, that is to say "Compass." Vinum was a very large purchaser of wine and was in the habit of financing its purchases by charging its purchases to Compass and other lenders. In the case of Compass there were master agreements to which both Vinum and the Company were parties the first dated in January 1974 and the second dated the 1st August 1974. They are both in the same form and I can refer to the latter which is exhibited to an Affidavit of Mr. Meech. The material part of it that follows is in the form of a letter of pledge addressed to Compass and it starts: "Gentlemen: In consideration of your lending to Vinum Limited ('Vinum') pursuant to a facility letter dated 18th January 1974 ('the Facility Letter') and thereby facilitating the payment by Vinum of the purchase price of certain wine purchased from London Wine Company (Shippers) Limited ('LWC'):– 1. Vinum hereby pledges the wine referred to in Schedule I attached to this letter and any further wine which may be the subject of a notice given to you in the form of Schedule II attached to this letter. 2. Vinum and LWC jointly and severally warrant the validity of the warehouse receipts and other documents evidencing the title to the wine referred to in paragraph 1 above ('the Wine')." 3 is a joint and several warrant of the market value, and I do not think I need read that. "4. Vinum warrants that it has good title to all the Wine and LWC warrants that so much of the Wine as was held to its order immediately prior to pledge pursuant to paragraph 1 above was held by LWC as custodian for Vinum. 5. The Wine and the proceeds of all insurances thereon and all sales thereof shall be a continuing security for the repayment to you of all or any sums due to you pursuant to the Facility Letter and this Letter of Pledge." 6. I do not think I need read. "7. Vinum undertakes to pay or procure the payment of all rent and other costs of and incidental to the storage and preservation of the Wine. 8. Vinum undertakes to maintain, at its cost, insurance in respect of the Wine against such risks and of such amount as you may from time to time require and will promptly pay all premiums on any policy in respect of the Wine taken out in your name. 9. Vinum requests LWC to discharge its obligations under paragraph 7 and 8 above as its agent and LWC agrees to discharge such obligations as agents for Vinum." 10 simply defines when the money becomes due, and 11 is a covenant of further assurance in the following terms: "Vinum and LWC undertake to sign execute and deliver any documents and to do anything which you may require for perfecting your title in the Wine or in vesting the same or delivering the same to any purchaser or purchasers from you."

The Second Schedule which is the form, it will be remembered, for pledging future wine is in these terms: "We Vinum Limited hereby pledge the wines described below subject to the terms of the Letter of Pledge dated January 28, 1974. We enclose the relative warehouse receipts in your favour together with copies of the instructions to the warehouse and evidence of title to the wine of the person giving those instructions. Vinum Limited and London Wine Company (Shippers) Limited jointly and severally warrant that the wines described below have an open market value at least as great as the invoiced price shown against the names of those wines and give in respect of such wines all the warranties and undertakings given in the said Letter of Pledge." Then there follow descriptions of the wines which are comprised in it.

There was also a special agreement between Vinum Ltd. and the Company regarding insurances and dated 28th January, 1974. It recites that Vinum would retain the facility with Compass, and that the Company would act as purchasing agents and wine investment counsel for Vinum Ltd. in connection with these purchases. It recites that funds were made available through the facility. It recites that under the terms and conditions in the Letter of Pledge to which the Company and Vinum were parties, as well as the terms and conditions of the facility, Vinum is obligated to maintain insurance on all its wines in bond which are pledged to Compass. "Now, therefore, Vinum Ltd. appoint the Company as its agents for procuring all necessary insurances on wines pledged by Vinum to Compass, or purchased or held by the Company or Vinum Ltd. with a view towards pledge by Vinum Ltd. to Compass."

As the wines were pledged to Compass so the warehouseman issued warehouse receipts in the form which I have previously described and sent to Compass letters of confirmation. Some of these are exhibited as typical. There is a letter, for instance, of 6th September 1974: "With reference to your letter of 30th August and our telephone conversation of today we can confirm that we are holding all the wines as listed in your letter in your name, this is according to our stock records and without physical check." There is another one in February from another warehouse. The first one I read was, I think, from Porter and Laker. This one is from the Isis Shipping Company. It says: "We confirm that we are holding the wine listed on our attached Warehouse receipts to the order of Compass Bank S.A., and will not release any of these wines from storage without written instructions from the authorised signatory of your Bank."

It is clear that some, at least, of the warehouse receipts exhibited in this case refer to cases of wine by reference numbers, but it has not been suggested either that this enables individual cases to be identified in the bulk or that any appropriation has taken place. At any rate so far as this summons is concerned, the questions raised by the summons are by definition restricted to cases where it is common ground that no act of appropriation had taken place before the relevant date, and the case has throughout been argued on the footing that no specific identification of goods attributable to particular purchase is possible.

After the summons was issued it was amended to add a purchaser in a fourth category, but as a result of what emerged at the hearing, I think it is in the event now unnecessary to deal with it. This category consists of purchasers in respect of whose orders wine was not only allocated but segregated and appropriated (so that the goods became ascertained goods) but whose goods cannot now be identified because they have been mixed with other batches of similar wine. Mr. Bingham on behalf of the Bank, however, has (clearly rightly, if I may say) conceded that this would not have the effect of reversing the property or giving the Bank any charge on the wine of purchasers in this category, and I need say no more about it at the moment.

There, then, are the three categories with which I have to deal and the question which has arisen in each case is whether the wines which have been sold belong to the purchasers and those claiming through or under them or whether on the relevant date they remained the Company's property and so became subject to the charge in the Debenture which then crystallised. I should perhaps say that there is no question of stocks being insufficient to fulfil all the purchase orders so that there is no competition between purchasers *inter se*.

The question is easier to pose than to answer and I am indebted to Counsel for all the respondents for sustained and instructive arguments. It will, I think, be convenient to deal with these in a different order from that in which they were advanced, because there are certain arguments common to all three cases which, if accepted, would render it unnecessary to consider the special features applicable to any particular case.

As regards the case of Mr. Strong and Mr. Button Mr. Wright's primary submission on their behalf is that the legal title to the goods passed and that, accordingly, the matter ends there. If, however, that is wrong, he submits first that the goods became subject to a valid and effective trust before the relevant date, and, as an alternative to this, that each purchaser had, before the relevant date, a right to specific performance of his contract and that, when the floating charge crystallised, the Bank took subject to that right. These two submissions apply equally to the third category and have been adopted and expanded by Mr. Stamler on behalf of the Respondents Vinum & Compass and since they are, therefore, common to all cases, and, if correct, are conclusive of the whole case, they can conveniently be dealt with first. As regards the creation of a trust, this is put in this way. On the assumption that no property passed in the goods at law—and it is not argued that this could possibly be the case in the third category represented by Mr. Bailey and by Mr. Stamler's clients—there was, it is submitted, clearly an intention that the property should pass so far as the Company had it in its power to make it do so. One has only to look at the terms of its circulars with their references to "*your* wines," to the purchaser being "the beneficial owner" and to the Company having a lien. This is reinforced when one looks at the terms of the letters of confirmation which list the quantities and types of wine and confirm that the purchaser is "the sole beneficial owner of these wines," and is indeed further reinforced in the case of Compass and Vinum when reference is made to the master agreements with Compass and the Company where the Company joins in to warrant title to the wine. By issuing these documents, the acknowledged purpose of which was to enable the purchasers to deal with their wines by sale or charge, the Company, it is said, evinced the clearest possible intention to declare itself a trustee and once you find such an intention, it matters not that the instrument expressing it fails to do so in unequivocal terms or, indeed, that there is no instrument at all. Reliance is placed upon the recent case of *Re Kayford* [1975 1 W.L.R. 279] where Mr. Justice Megarry said "It is well settled that a trust can be created without using the words 'trust' or 'confidence' or the like: the question is whether in substance a sufficient intention trust has been manifested."

That, of course, is a proposition with which it is impossible to quarrel but I do not find that case, where the evidence of intention to create a trust was exceptionally clear and where the trust property was from the outset specifically set aside and identified, one which assists me very much in ascertaining whether, in the very different circumstances of the instant case, a trust has been effectively declared. Mr. Wright, in his reply, put it rather differently. A trust, he said, may be constituted not merely by direct and express declaration but also by the consequences flowing from the acts of the persons themselves to which consequences the law attaches the label "trust." A trust, to put it another way, is the technical description of a legal situation; and where you find (i) an intention to create a beneficial interest in someone else (ii) an acknowledgment of that intention and (iii) property in the ownership of the person making the acknowledgment which answers the description in the acknowledgment, then there is, at the date of the acknowledgment, an effective and completed trust of all the property of the acknowledger answering to that description. This is, I think, in essence the same submission as that made by Mr. Stamler—he submits that where one is dealing with a homogeneous mass there is no problem about certainty, So long as the mass can be identified and there is no uncertainty about the quantitative interest of the Beneficiary the Court will find no difficulty in administering the trust if it once finds the necessary intention to create an equitable interest in property of the type comprised in the mass. I think, indeed, that if the case is to be made out at all, it must be put in this way, for the submission itself is based on the premise that there are no specific or ascertained goods in which the beneficiary is interested. Were it otherwise there would be no need to invoke the concept of trust for the title would have passed under the Sale of Goods Act (as, indeed, Mr. Wright submits in categories 1 and 2, it did). If trust there be, then it must be a trust of the homogeneous *whole* and the terms of the trust must be that the trustee is to hold that whole upon trust to give effect thereout to the proportionate interest of the beneficiary. Thus if we postulate the case of the Company having in warehouse 1,000 cases of particular wine and selling 100 cases to X the circumstances of this case indicate, it is submitted, that the Company created an equitable tenancy in common between itself and X in the whole 1,000 cases in the proportions of 9/10ths and 1/10th.

It is with regret that I feel compelled to reject these submissions, for I feel great sympathy with those who paid for their wine and received an assurance that they had title to it. But I find it impossible to spell either out of the acknowledgments signed by the Company or out of the circumstances any such trust as is now sought to be set up. Granted that the references to "beneficial interest" are appropriate words for the creation of a trust; granted, even (although this I think is very difficult to spell out) that that was the Company's intention, it seems to me that any such trust must fail on the ground of uncertainty of subject matter. I appreciate the point taken that the subject matter is part of a homogeneous mass so that specific identity is of as little importance as it is, for instance, in the case of money. Nevertheless, as it seems to me, to create a trust it must be possible to ascertain with certainty not only what the interest of the beneficiary is to be but to what property it is to attach.

I cannot see how, for instance, a farmer who declares himself to be a trustee of two sheep (without identifying them) can be said to have created a perfect and complete trust whatever rights he may confer by such declaration as a matter of contract. And it would seem to me to be immaterial that at the time he has a flock of sheep out of which he could satisfy the interest. Of course, he could by appropriate words, declare himself to be a trustee of a specified proportion of his whole flock and thus create an equitable tenancy in common between himself and the named beneficiary, so that a proprietary interest would arise in the beneficiary in an undivided share of all the flock and its produce. But the *mere* declaration that a given number of animals would be held upon trust could not, I should have thought, without very clear words pointing to such an intention, result in the creation of an interest in common in the proportion which that number bears to the number of the whole at the time of the declaration. And where the mass from which the numerical interest is to take effect is not itself ascertainable at the date of the declaration such a conclusion becomes impossible.

In the instant case, even if I were satisfied on the evidence that the mass was itself identifiable at the date of the various letters of confirmation I should find the very greatest difficulty in construing the assertion that "you are the *sole* and beneficial owner of" 10 cases of such and such a wine as meaning or intended to mean "you are the owner of such proportion of the total stock of such and such a wine now held by me as 10 bears to the total number of cases comprised in such stock." All other things apart, such construction would be a total negation of the assertion "you are the *sole* owner." But in fact, (leaving aside the first category for the moment) it is far from clear what, at the date of any individual letter of confirmation, was the composition of the mass from which the interest was to take effect. It was suggested in argument that the words "lying in bond" on the invoice was a reference to the stocks held by the Company in bond at that date and that therefore it was possible to predicate of any individual letter of confirmation that it referred to cases forming part of a then existing mass. I do not think that these words signify that, but in any event it does not seem necessary to have been the case at all that there was an ascertainable existing mass at the time of the individual letter. For example, in the case of Mr. Bailey, the exhibited correspondence shows that a quantity of wines of various descriptions was invoiced on the 16th August 1972 and described as "lying in bond." At the same time the Company wrote to Mr. Bailey's bankers undertaking that the wines on the invoice "will not be removed from the Bond without your written authority." On the 29th September 1972 the bankers wrote to the Company asking for the warehouse warrants, and on the 6th October Mr. Baring replied saying that the wines had "now just arrived in the country." The warehouse receipts were actually sent on the 10th November, 1972. So that it appears that, at least in this case, the wines described as "lying in bond" in August were not in fact in the warehouse at all at that date.

Mr. Wright, however, draws support for his submissions from the decision of Sir John Romilly in *Pooley* v. *Budd* [14 Beav. 200]. This was a case which came before the Court on demurrer and the bill alleged that the Ystalyfera Iron Company, the Defendant, "was possessed of many hundred tons of" iron "including the iron particularly mentioned in" a document dated the 23rd July 1850 "and the same was, on the said 23rd July 1850, stacked upon the ironworks at Swansea." The Plaintiff then alleged a contract to sell one Scale (another Defendant) 250 tons of white and mottled pig iron and 250 tons of bright and grey pig iron against a bill of exchange drawn on one Dummler and accepted by him. The sellers sent to their London agents a document recording the sale and this was endorsed by the agents and handed to Scale against delivery of the bill of exchange.

The document which was dated the 23rd July 1850 was in these terms:–"We hold stacked on our wharf at Swansea 250 tons of white and mottled pig iron 250 tons of bright and grey ditto, 500 tons, all of our usual quality which we engage to deliver free on board at

Swansea to the bearer of this document only, on presentation endorsed by Messrs. H. Moss & Company" (the London agents) "we having been paid for the same."

Scale then purported to pledge the iron to the Plaintiff as security for a loan and the document was delivered to him. He wrote to the Defendant Company to make arrangements for the delivery of the iron and the Defendant Company replied saying that their shipping agent at Swansea had orders to honour the warrant and to deliver the iron to whoever presented it.

In the meantime, (so it was alleged) the bill of exchange was negotiated by the Defendant Company to a third party for value received by the Defendant Company, which, however refused to deliver the iron and sold it elsewhere. The relief claimed was a declaration that the iron was effectively charged with the loan, an account of the iron and its proceeds and payment over of the proceeds in satisfaction of the loan.

Sir John Romilly overruled the demurrer on the ground that the Defendant Company was a trustee of the iron. The case is sufficiently unusual to merit careful attention and it is interesting to note first that it came before the Court on demurrer so that all allegations in the bill were accepted as true and secondly that it was argued by counsel in support of the bill on two grounds, that is to say, estoppel and trust.

In the course of argument it was submitted that it was sufficiently averred that the iron had been severed from the rest because it was described as a particular quantity and quality "stacked on the Company's wharf at Swansea."

It seems clear that the case presented by counsel was on the footing that the iron was an identified chattel for they quoted the following passage from *Wood* v. *Rowcliffe*, [2 Ph. (Phil.) 382]: "The jurisdiction to protect by injunction the possession, and to decree the delivery up of *specific* chattels, is not confined to chattels, the loss or injury of which would not adequately be compensated by damages, but extends to all cases in which the party in possession of the chattels has acquired such possession through an alleged abuse of power on the part of one standing in a fiduciary relationship to the Plaintiff."

That fiduciary relationship, it was argued, arose by estoppel. At page 42 of the Report the Master of the Rolls made some preliminary observations before delivering judgment. He said: "I think the decision will turn upon the allegations as to the company being in such a position, that they must be treated as holding the goods with the complete ownership in Scale. I cannot doubt that a trust may be created in personal chattels and that this Court would execute it; and that on a mere sale of goods this Court will not interfere, but leave the parties to proceed at law. If there was a complete and perfect ownership in Scale, the whole of the purchase-money having been paid, the company could only be considered as holders of the goods in trust for him, and he having given a lien in favour of the Plaintiff, I should think that this demurrer could not be sustained. If it was only a lien on the unperformed contract, he must stand in the same situation as Scale, and if Scale could not come into a Court of Equity the Plaintiff cannot."

He delivered judgment, I think, about a week later, and at page 43 he says this: "The principles affecting these cases are now well settled in Courts of Equity. On the one hand, it is and has long been the law of this Court, that it will not lend its assistance to enforce the specific performance of ordinary contracts for the sale and purchase of personal chattels, unless, as in the case of *Buxton* v. *Lister* (3 Atk. 383), there be something very special in the nature of the contract. On the other hand, if a trust be created, the circumstance that the subject-matter to which the trust is attached is a personal chattel, will not prevent this Court from enforcing the due execution of that trust."

At page 44 he says: "Trusts, however, may be constituted not merely by direct declaration of trust, but also by constructive operation of the consequence flowing from the acts of the persons themselves. Thus, equity will not merely enforce the execution of a trust against the trustees themselves, but against all persons who obtain possession of the property affected by the trust, provided they had notice of the trust. So if, in this case, Scale had been the agent of the Plaintiff, and had paid for the iron with the Plaintiff's money, this Court would have held Scale to be the trustee of the iron for the Plaintiff, and would have compelled him to deliver the iron to him, or make him account for the proceeds of the sale of it, if it had been disposed of; and it would, in like manner, have compelled any person to do the same, who had acquired the property from Scale, if that person had been aware of the circumstances under which Scale had himself obtained possession of the property in the first instance."

At page 45 he says this: "It is therefore important to bear in mind, in this case, that as equity would not enforce the specific performance of the contract for the sale and delivery of the iron, the relation of trustee and *cestui que trust* cannot spring merely from the contract, and that, if it exists at all, it must be shown to exist from something beyond the mere contract entered into between the company and Scale for the sale and delivery of iron. At the same time, if the contract were complete so far as the company were concerned—that is to say, if they had been paid every penny they were entitled to, and if they had no claim upon or interest in the iron arising from the contract, and the contract only remained unperformed to this extent, that the iron had not been delivered to the purchaser—I should entertain no doubt, but that the company would then and thereby, become mere trustees of the iron sold, for the benefit of the real purchaser or the person entitled to claim it under him. To constitute this relation of trustee and *cestui que trust*, therefore, in this case, I think that two things must be established; first that the actual property or chattel existed to which the trust is to be attached, at the time when, if ever, the relation of trustee and *cestui que trust* arose; and secondly, that the company, the actual possessor of the goods, had "no ownership or property existing in those goods."

At page 46 there is, I think, an important observation, because he says this: "There are, in my opinion, sufficient allegations to show, that the bill treats and proceeds upon the assertion of the existence of the particular property in question at the time of the contract. That it was not severed by the company from the rest of their stock is not material: it is alleged to have existed *in specie* on their wharf at the time of the contract, and if they had not any ownership in that *particular* property, but held it merely in trust for the owner, the circumstance that they have since parted with it, either alone or together with the rest of their then existing stock, or that they have mixed it up with their stock and cannot now distinguish it, will not take away the right of the Plaintiff to enforce the execution of a trust which they made themselves liable to perform." He goes on to say: "I think that the contract cannot be said to have been completed, if any interest in the iron remained in them arising out of the contract. . . . If these allegations are true, and for this purpose they are to be taken as such, I think that the company had no property or right of ownership in the iron so stacked on their wharf, and so sold to the Defendant Scale."

At page 48 he says: "I am of opinion, that, taking all the allegations in this bill to be correct, the company must, by their own admission, be taken to have ceased to have any interest in the iron, at the time when Budd signed that bought note, and at the time when that lien was created. The iron was an existing quantity stacked on their wharf, though not severed. If these facts were proved, I think I should be bound "to hold that, although the company might be creditors of Scale, they were mere naked trustees of this iron, denuded of all interest in it, and that this is not a bill to enforce specific performance of a contract for the sale of a chattel."

In so far as this decision suggests that the property in goods sold by generic description can pass before the goods are ascertained it cannot, I think, stand—nor does Mr. Wright contend that it can—against other more authoritative decisions or against the express provisions of section 16 of the Sale of Goods Act 1893 and he relies upon it only to show that the mere fact that property is the subject-matter of a contract of sale between vendor and vendee does not necessarily oust the possibility that, in appropriate circumstances, the former may constitute himself a trustee for the latter. He points, however, to the fact that, for aught that appears, the goods in that case were no more ascertained than they were in the instant case. I am not sure, in fact that that is so because although it is true that the Master of the Rolls seems to have considered severance irrelevant, it does appear from the passages in the judgment which I have read that he was looking not at a real situation but at the somewhat artificial question of what was the allegation in the bill and he concluded that there was a sufficient allegation of an identifiable quantity stacked in a particular place. It was, he said, "alleged to have existed *in specie* on their wharf at the time of the contract and if they had not any ownership in that *particular* property, but held it merely in trust for the owner" subsequent dealings would not destroy the Plaintiffs' right to have the trust executed. On that supposition, the fact that they negotiated Scales' bill was sufficient to destroy any lien that they might otherwise have claimed.

I cannot, therefore, regard this case as authority for the proposition that a trust can effectively be created in unascertained chattels or that a trust arises from an uncompleted contract for the sale of goods merely because the Vendor has been paid and has acknowledged the buyer's right to delivery. Indeed such a proposition would, as it seems to me, be a negation of what Lord Shaw in *Bank of Scotland* v. *Macleod*, [1914 A.C. 311] and page 337, called "the well settled principle that a contractual obligation with regard to property which has not effectually and actually brought about either a security upon it or a conveyance of it is not *per se* the foundation of a trust or of a declarator of trust."

Nor do I think that if, in fact, Sir John Romilly's proposition was that a trust was created of unascertained goods, *Porley* v. *Budd* can stand today in the light of the decision of the Court of Appeal in *In re Wait* [1927 1 Ch 606]. That was a claim for specific performance of a contract for the sale of goods and it raised two questions, both of which may conveniently be dealt with here since that relating to specific performance also bears upon submissions made in the instant case to which I shall advert a little later. The essential facts can be stated very shortly. *Wait*, in whose bankruptcy the question arose, had agreed under a c.i.f. contract to purchase 1,000 tons of wheat ex motor vessel Challenger expected to load between particular dates from either Oregon or Washington. He subsold under another c.i.f. contract 500 tons of this parcel to the respondents. The wheat was duly shipped in bulk and a bill of lading for the 1,000 tons was issued and received by Wait. Wait invoiced the respondents and was paid by them for their 500 tons except for their proportion of the freight. He then hypothecated the bill of lading to the bank to secure his overdraft. Subsequently he was adjudicated bankrupt on his own petition and a special manager was appointed to whom the respondents tendered the freight. He returned it and subsequently, having discharged the indebtedness to the bank, received from the bank the bill of lading. The 1,000 tons remained in bulk and no appropriation had taken place of the 500 tons purchased by the Respondents. They, however, issued a Notice of Motion in the Bristol County Court claiming that the Official Receiver should be ordered by way of specific performance to deliver 500 out of the 1,000 tons to them on payment of £750, their proportion of the freight. They asked for alternative relief including a declaration that they had a beneficial interest in the parcel of 1,000 tons to the extent of 500 tons. There remained 530 tons at the date of the Motion, the 500 tons still being unappropriated. The Divisional Court in bankruptcy, reversing the County Court judge on this point, held that the goods were specific and ordered specific performance, but this was reversed by the Court of Appeal. The claim for specific performance was made in reliance upon section 52 of the Sale of Goods Act 1893 (which replaced section 2 of the Mercantile Law Amendment Act 1856) and is in these terms: "In any action for breach of contract to deliver specific or ascertained goods the Court may, if it thinks fit, on the application of the plaintiff by its judgment direct that the contract shall be performed specifically without giving the defendant the option of retaining the goods on payment of damages." It was assumed both by the Court and by the very eminent Counsel who appeared in the case that any jurisdiction to order specific performance arose from this section and this section alone and the only question with which the Court was concerned so far as this limb of the argument was concerned was whether the goods were specific or ascertained.

But there was an alternative argument based upon equitable assignment and it is interesting to see how it was put, because in substance it comes to the same thing as the submission made in the instant case, for although both Counsel and the Court spoke of "equitable assignment" it is clear that the essence of the submission was that a fully paid vendor became a trustee of the property in the whole cargo to give effect to a proprietary interest of the purchaser in part. At page 612 of the Report we find Mr. Luxmoore (as he then was) for the Respondents saying this: "Further there was a good equitable assignment to the respondents. As soon as the respondents had paid their purchase money, Wait became a trustee for them. . . . Every payment in part performance of a contract transfers to the purchaser in equity a corresponding portion of the property. . . . Here the equity attached to the 1,000 tons and operated to restrain dealing with them except subject to the provision of the 500 tons for the respondents. The purchaser of a portion of a cargo obtains an undivided interest in the whole cargo . . . which is an insurable interest."

Lord Hanworth summarised the contentions at page 615. He says: "This was the point mainly relied upon in this Court, for counsel for the respondents to the appeal did not contend that there was any trust as to the £5,933, or that he could claim to follow the money on the basis of a trust, expressed or implied. His contention was (a) that although the 500 tons were not identified and agreed upon at the time the contract of sale was made so as to satisfy the term 'specific goods' as interpreted under s.62 of the Code, yet they were 'ascertained goods' within s.52, after the wheat had been shipped on board the motor vessel Challenger, for they could be, and therefore ought to be ascertained from out of the wheat bought from Balfour Williamson & Co., at any rate upon arrival at Avonmouth, and (b) that on payment of the purchase price there was an equitable assignment of so much of the wheat ex motor vessel Challenger as was necessary to satisfy the contract to sell 500 tons on which the payment had been made."

After reviewing the authorities and rejecting the argument on specific performance, he deals with the arguments based upon equitable assignment at page 623 where he quotes from the speech of Lord Cranworth in the case of *Hoare* v. *Dresser*, [7 Ho. Lords C. 317]. What Lord Cranworth said was this: "But I apprehend that neither in equity nor in law can there be any jurisdiction to say, that because there is property of the person who ought to have fulfilled his contract, therefore you can make that property available for the specific performance of the engagement." Lord Hanworth goes on: "The requisite is that the subject-matter of the contract must have become specific. Looking then at the present case more particularly from the point of view of equitable assignment, the sub-purchasers cannot fulfil the conditions necessary to give them such a right. Lord Wensleydale in *Hoare* v. *Dresser* says: 'I take it to be perfectly clear that in order to create an equitable assignment, the obligation must be to deliver a particular chattel, not to deliver any chattel.' The doctrine of equitable assignment of goods is discussed by Lord Selborne in the case of *Citizens' Bank of Louisiana* v. *First National Bank of New Orleans* in relation to funds remitted to meet bills of exchange upon the bankruptcy of the drawer. In that case the evidence was that one of the bills was drawn specially against funds. Lord Selbourne asks: 'Is that an equitable assignment? Is that an appropriation of such a kind, that from the moment when that transaction took place as between the two banks, the Citizens' Bank would become purchasers *pro tanto*, to the amount necessary to answer this bill drawn at sixty days' sight, of previous remittances made by the drawers to their agents at Liverpool, in order to provide for that and other bills which they might draw? My Lords, it seems to me that the transaction is simply one of the most ordinary mercantile kind, and perfectly consistent with the ordinary course of dealing between the Liverpool Bank and the drawers of the bills, which upon the whole of the correspondence and the evidence plainly was not one of specific trust or appropriation of any particular funds. The transaction was really of this kind—a person asked to take a bill wants to know distinctly whether the person who has drawn it has made provision for its payment. The statement is, we have sent forward to Liverpool funds of a much larger amount, which are intended to be used in the payment of these and other bills. My Lords, if that be a specific appropriation or an equitable assignment, it follows that every ordinary transaction in commerce, where any inquiry whatever is made, would come into the same category.' " And Lord Hanworth adds: "And see also *Field* v. *Megaw* where specific appropriation is referred to by Montague Smith J. as necessary to bind the fund by equitable assignment."

Lord Atkin (Lord Justice Atkin as he then was) at page 630 says this as regards, first of all, the claim for specific performance "This claim of the claimants to specific performance in their argument in the Courts below and before us was based solely on the provisions of s.52 of the Sale of Goods Act, 1893." He then deals with the meaning of "specific" and "ascertained" goods, and he concludes: "Speaking generally, Courts of equity did not decree specific performance in contracts for the sale of commodities which could be ordinarily obtained in the market where damages were a sufficient remedy. Possibly the statutory remedy was intended to be available even in those cases. But the Code appears to have this effect, that in contracts for the sale of goods the only remedy by way of specific performance is the statutory remedy, and it follows that as the goods were neither specific nor ascertained the remedy of specific performance was not open to the creditors."

As regards the argument on equitable assignment, he deals with that at page 634, and he says: "I now proceed to discuss the suggestion that apart from the right to specific performance under s.52 of the Code, there was in this case an equitable assignment to the claimant of 500 tons of flour which entitled them to claim from the trustee delivery of 500 tons out of the 530 tons remaining in his possession, and, indeed, gave the claimant a charge or lien over the whole 1,000 tons to which the debtor was entitled under his contract with Balfour Williamson & Co. In the view that I have taken of the facts of this case, I have already said that the goods were never so ascertained that specific performance could have been ordered of them. This consideration would appear to defeat the supposed equitable assignment, and I will not repeat the passages referred to by the Master of the Rolls which establish the test. I have already indicated my own view of the claimants' contract of November 21 and suggested that the debtor does not in fact agree to sell to the claimants any aliquot part of the 1,000 tons, which in fact he had agreed to buy from Balfour Williamson & Co. But even if he had, I do not think that at any time here there was an equitable assignment which ever gave the claimants a beneficial interest in these goods. It has been difficult to elicit the moment of time at which the beneficial interest came into existence. At various times in the argument it has been the moment when the 1,000 tons were shipped: when they were declared to the debtor by Balfour Williamson & Co.; when the bills of lading came into the possession of the bank; when the claimants paid the £5,933.5s. to the debtor; when the goods were taken up by the trustee; and when the 530 tons came into the possession of the trustee. The difficulty illustrates the danger of seeking to conduct well established principles into territory where they are trespassers. Without deciding the point, I think that much may be said for the proposition that an agreement for the sale of goods does not import any agreement to transfer property other than in accordance with the terms of the Code, that is, the intention of the parties to be derived from the terms of the contract, the conduct of the parties and the circumstances of the case, and, unless a different intention appears, from the rules set out in s.18. The Code was passed at a time when the principles of equity and equitable remedies were recognised and given effect to in all our Courts, and the particular equitable remedy of specific performance is specially referred to in s.52."

At page 636 he goes on: "The rules for transfer of property as between seller and buyer, performance of the contract, rights of the unpaid seller against the goods, unpaid sellers' lien, remedies of the seller, remedies of the buyer, appear to be complete and exclusive statements of the legal relations both in law and equity. They have, of course, no relevance when one is considering rights, legal or equitable, which may come into existence dehors the contract for sale. A seller or a purchaser may, of course, create any equity he pleases by way of charge, equitable assignment or any other dealing with or disposition of goods, the subject-matter of sale; and he may, of course, create such an equity as one of the terms expressed in the contract of sale. But the mere sale or agreement to sell or the acts in pursuance of such a contract mentioned in the Code will only produce the legal effects which the Code states.

"But without deciding this point, we have to apply the words of Lord Westbury in *Holroyd* v. *Marshall*: 'In equity it is not necessary for the alienation of property that there should be a formal deed of conveyance. A contract for valuable consideration, by which it is agreed to make a present transfer of property, passes at once the beneficial interest, provided the contract is one of which a Court of equity will decree specific performance. In the language of Lord Hardwicke, the vendor becomes a trustee for the vendee; subject, of course, to the contract being one to be specifically performed. And this is true, not only of contracts relating to real estate, but also of contracts relating to personal property, provided that the latter are such as a Court of equity would direct to be specifically performed.' " Lord Atkin goes on: "It must be remembered that while Lord Westbury's proposition that a contract for valuable consideration, by which it is agreed to make a present transfer of property, passes at once, the beneficial interest, provided the contract is one of which a Court of equity will decree specific performance, may be beyond dispute, the converse that when there is a contract of which the Court of equity will decree specific performance the beneficial interest has passed is not logically true, and is not the law. Nor is it true that in equity when a man agrees in a contract for the sale of goods to sell part of a specified whole, he agrees to make a transfer of property either present or when the property is in fact acquired. Agreements by a farmer to sell a lamb out of his flock, a ton of potatoes out of his crop grown on his farm, a bushel of apples from his orchard, a gallon of milk from this morning's milking, an egg out of the eggs collected yesterday, seems to me not to amount to an equitable assignment of any of the matter sold, or to give an equitable charge or lien over the whole subject-matter to secure the delivery of the part. The doctrine asserted seems to produce the result that in every case of the sale of future goods, as soon as the goods have become identifiable, the beneficial interest in them passes to the buyer, notwithstanding the provision in the Code that, in the absence of express intention, the property only passes when goods of that description and in a deliverable state are appropriated to the contract. . . . So to hold," he goes on, "would be to defeat the intention of the parties, either express or to be implied from their contract being bound by the terms of the Code, and it appears to me not to accord with the principles of equity to impose upon the parties rights which are contrary to their manifest intention."

And then he asks: "Does it make any difference that the creditors here paid their purchase money in advance of the due date, and in any case before they could get delivery under the contract? I think not." After dealing with specific performance and referring to Lord Westbury's statement in *Holroyd* v. *Marshall*, he says: "I cannot help thinking that in his reference to property real or personal, the learned Lord was not directing his mind to contracts for the sale of goods which ordinarily would not be 'of the class of which a Court of equity would decree the specific performance.' I cannot believe he intended that in the cases suggested above the farmer, the seller, would hold the lamb, or the potatoes or the bushel of apples or the egg in trust for the purchaser as soon as they were ascertained, much less, as these words are supposed to mean, as soon as they were acquired by the seller. Similarly, I fail to see how the payment of the price can convert that which was not an equitable assignment before the payment, into an equitable assignment after the payment. Payment of the price has no doubt been material in considering a different question—namely, the right of the purchaser in a contract for the sale of real property, who pays the price or portion of the price before conveyance, to be given a lien on the land for his purchase price. The right is correlative to and appears to be derived from the right of the unpaid vendor of real property to claim a lien on the land after conveyance for the unpaid purchase price. But the latter lien in my judgment does not exist in the case of an ordinary sale of goods. The remedies are defined." As it seems to me, this reasoning is equally conclusive of the argument as to the creation of a trust which has been advanced in the instant case.

The other argument which is advanced in all three categories is that the contract between the Company and its purchasers is one which conferred upon the purchasers, in all the circumstances, a right of specific performance. That right, it is said affected the goods when the Bank's charge under the debenture crystallised and the Bank, therefore, acquired its charge over the goods subject to the purchasers' rights to have their contracts specifically performed. *Re Wait*, to which I have just referred, is an obvious difficulty in the way of such a submission, but it is said that the case was one concerned only with the statutory right conferred by section 52 of the Sale of Goods Act. And indeed I have already referred to the passages in the judgments which deal with that. There is, it is argued, a general power to decree specific performance of a contract for the sale of goods where damages would not be an adequate remedy which exists independently of the statute and which does not depend upon the goods being specific or ascertained. The existence of such a right is, it is said, demonstrated by the recent case of *Sky Petroleum Ltd.* v. *V.I.P.* [1974 1 All E.R. 954]. I can, I think, deal with this submission very shortly, for it seems to me that even if the case cited establishes the existence of a power in the Court to decree specific performance of a contract for the sale of goods in cases not covered by section 52—and, the contract in that case was not, I think, itself a sale of goods but a long-term supply contract under which successive sales would arise if orders were placed and accepted—the existence of such a power cannot help the Respondents in the present case. It could do so only if the existence of the right established some proprietary interest in the goods to which they were subject at the date when the charge crystallised. But one thing that is common ground here is that the goods never were ascertained and *Re Wait* shows that no lien arises from the mere payment of the purchase price. As Lord Atkin pointed out it is not the law that whenever there is a contract of which equity will decree specific performance a beneficial interest in the subject-matter of the contract passes as a necessary corollary, Even if, therefore, specific performance could be decreed of the purchasers' contracts in the instant case, the decree could not affect any specific goods in the Company's possession, for under the contracts the goods were never ascertained, and leaving aside any question of notice, I do not see how the possibility of a decree against the Company for the delivery *in specie* of so many cases of wine could affect the Bank merely because it happened to have a charge over wine of that description which the Company had acquired but never appropriated to the contract.

The position in such a case is, I think, quite different from that which arose in *George Barker (Transport) Ltd.* v. *Eynon* [1974 1 All E.R. 900] on which Mr. Stamler relied, for there the claim was to a lien on specific goods which were in the plaintiffs' possession.

I turn now, therefore, to the submissions peculiar to the individual cases. Now in the case of Mr. Strong, although the goods were sold by generic description, it happened that at the material time the quantity described was in the Company's possession and was the only wine of that description in its possession, although it is not claimed that it could not, without undue difficulty, obtain additional quantities from elsewhere if it required to do so. Mr. Wright argues that the result of this was to ascertain the goods and that the property passed; and to make this good he has to rely either upon section 17 or upon an appropriation under section 18 Rule 5 (1) of the Sale of Goods Act. Section 16 states quite clearly that the property is not transferred to the buyer unless and until the goods are ascertained but it is not a necessary corollary of this that the property *does* pass to the buyer when they *are* ascertained. To produce that result one either has had to find an appropriation (from which an intention to pass the property will be inferred) or one has to find an intention manifested in some other way. Mr. Wright relies upon what has been referred to as an "ascertainment by exhaustion" and has drawn my attention to the decision of Mr. Justice Roche in *Wait & James* v. *Midland Bank*, [31 Com. Cas., 172]. That was an interpleader between the unpaid vendor of goods and a Bank to whom the goods had been pledged by the purchasers. There were three separate contracts for quantities of a specified bulk of wheat, the quantities being respectively 250, 750 and 250 quarters. The purchasers had themselves obtained delivery of 400 quarters and there came a time when, as a result of successive sales and deliveries, there remained out of the bulk in the warehouse only 850 quarters. The sale notes in the case of all three contracts were in substantially the same form and recorded a sale of "so many quarters of Australian Wheat at 62s, 496 lbs ex store Avonmouth ex Thistleros." A delivery note of the same date was addressed to the warehouseman and directed them to "deliver ex Thistleros ex Store" to the Purchasers. Mr. Justice Roche found as a fact that by the 16th

November 1925 the whole cargo ex Thistleros (all of which was owned by the sellers originally) had been delivered with the exception of 850 quarters.

At page 179 of the report he says this: "In my judgment, the matter has been dealt with automatically by the facts, and the facts have provided the method of ascertainment in the manner I have already described through the delivery of the rest of the goods to other purchasers. I therefore hold that what remains in the warehouse has been ascertained to be the quantity of goods agreed to be sold by Messrs. Wait and James to Messrs. Redlers Limited, and to be the goods transferred by Messrs. Redlers, Limited, to the Midland Bank. It remains to consider one other argument based upon the construction of section 16 of the Sale of Goods Act. There are here three contracts, and the section provides as follows: 'Where there is a contract for the sale of unascertained goods, no property in the goods is transferred to the buyer unless and until the goods are ascertained.' The claimants contend that there has been no differentiation or ascertainment of distinct goods as being either the goods dealt with under the contract of September 25, or of the goods dealt with and comprised under the contract of October 1, or those dealt with under the Contract of October 13. This objection is well founded in fact; but I think that it is altogether too narrow a construction of the section. These contracts were always in one hand. That is to say, they were all sales to Messrs. Redlers Limited, and they were all transferred to the bank, and I cannot imagine unless there were sub-divisions, that there would be any weighing taking place under circumstances which would stop with breaks of 250, 750, or 250, and I cannot conceive that if there were not such breaks in weighing if it took place that it would be said: 'Well, you have ascertained that there are 6,800 quarters here, but you have never ascertained what is left under each particular one of these contracts. In my judgment it is sufficient if, where there are contracts for the sale of unascertained goods to one buyer, it is ascertained what the goods are which are covered by those contracts; and I hold that this is the permissible and proper construction of section 16.' "

The decision in that case was one of obvious common sense because in fact from November 16th onwards there were no goods from which the seller could have fulfilled the contracts except the 850 quarters. They could, no doubt, have delivered 850 quarters of Australian Wheat but not 850 quarters "ex store Avonmouth ex Thistleros." The instant case seems to me quite different. It is not and cannot be alleged that the sale to Mr. Strong was a sale of specific goods. What the Company undertook to do was to deliver so many cases and bottles of the specified type of wine "lying in bond." This does not in my judgment link the wine sold with any given consignment or warehouse. The fact that the Company had at the date of the invoice that amount of wine and that amount only is really irrelevant to the contract. No doubt it could have fulfilled the order from this wine but it could equally have fulfilled it from any other source. It is not contended that there was any act of appropriation and Mr. Wright's case is that the property passed under s.17 when the usual title letter mentioning the wine described in the invoice was sent some three months later, by which date, he says, the wine was ascertained. I cannot draw that conclusion from the material before me, for it seems to me clear that the Company was, under the contract, at liberty to deliver to the purchaser any bottles of wine which tallied with the description. It never has been,therefore, to use Mr. Justice Roche's words, ascertained what the goods are which are covered by the contract.

The argument in relation to the second category of case is very similar. It will be remembered that in the *Wait & James* case Mr. Justice Roche restricts his remarks to the case of one buyer under several contracts. It is, however, submitted that where you have several buyers under several contracts, then, when you reach a stage where the totality of those contracted quantities exhausts the whole of the mass from which the individual contracts are to be fulfilled, there is no longer any property in the seller but the buyers own the mass as tenants in common.

The cases principally relied upon in support of this submission were *Spence* v. *Union Marine Insurance*, [L.R. 3 C.P.R. 42], and *Inglis* v. *Stock*, [10 App. Cas. 263]. The former is of little help because it was concerned with a wholly different question, namely, what is the result when specific goods which undoubtedly were in separate individual ownerships to start with become so mixed as to be indistinguishable. *Inglis* v. *Stock*, however, does contain some expressions of opinion which give apparent support to the contention. The action was one under an insurance policy in respect of sugar shipped from Hamburg "free on board." The loss sued on was the loss of 200 tons which the Plaintiff had purchased from a sugar merchant in Hamburg. He was also the sub-purchaser of a further quantity of 200 tons although this was not known to the sellers. It appears to have been the practice in the trade to ship sugar for several consignees in bulk and without any appropriation of the individual contract, taking bills of lading of small quantities and allocating those bills among the various purchasers in England, after shipment, according to the analysed saccharine content of the sugar. The whole consignment having been lost and the Plaintiff having insured the question was whether he had an insurable interest in the goods. The case was not directly concerned with property rights because the assumption was that the Plaintiff had no property in the sugar and the inquiry in the Court of Appeal centred round the meaning which could be given to the expression "free on board" in the case of unappropriated goods. The contract was construed as one under which the risk of loss fell on the purchaser (so that he remained liable for the price) and it was held accordingly that since he stood to make a financial loss, he had an insurable interest. The relevance of the case in the present context really arises entirely from the remarks made in the speech of Lord Selborne at page 267 where he said this: "It is contended on the part of the appellant, that, under these circumstances, and for want of a proper division before the loss, the shipment had not the effect of divesting the prior title of Drake & Co., the vendors, or of passing any interest in these sugars to the plaintiff. This argument appears to me to confound two very different things; the appropriation necessary as between vendor and purchaser, and the division, as between purchaser and purchaser, of specific goods, actually appropriated to the aggregate of the two contracts. I do not think it follows that there could be no appropriation by the vendor of which the purchasers might take the benefit, merely because the parcels of goods appropriated were mixed, in the act of appropriation, so as to require some subsequent division or apportionment. Whether this may have happened by previous agreement of course of dealing between all the parties (in which case there could be no serious doubt), or by accident, error, or want of proper care on the vendor's part, appears to me to make no difference in principle. The purchasers might possibly be entitled to reject, but the vendors could not, in my opinion, without their consent retract the appropriation."

"In the present case, I see no reason to doubt that the difficulty arising from the confusion of parcels—material only to the settlement of the amounts payable by the plaintiff to his two vendors—if not solved by consent (or by arbitration, for which each contract provided) would have been soluble by principles of law, applied to the facts and the terms of the contracts." But the question at issue in that case was not the passing of the property but the passing of the risk and that is made quite clear at page 270 by Lord Blackburn. He says this: "In case of an insurance on goods, if he," that is the purchaser, "shows that he had at the time of the loss the whole legal property in the goods which were lost, he undoubtedly does show it. But I do not agree that this is the only way in which he can show an insurable interest in goods, or that any relation to goods such that if the goods perish on the voyage the person will lose the whole, and if they arrive safe will have all or part of the goods, will not give an interest which may be aptly described as goods."

It is true that he goes on at page 274 to speak of an undivided interest in the goods, but I doubt very much whether he was using the word "interest" in the sense of a proprietary interest in the goods themselves, and it is worth referring to the analysis of Lord Justice

Scrutton in *Sterns Ltd.* v. *Vickers Ltd.* [1923 1 K.B. 78] at page 84 where he says this: "The question as to the effect of such a sale of an undivided portion of a larger bulk has frequently arisen in the Courts, and was much discussed in the well-known case of *Inglis* v. *Stock* where a similar argument to that which was addressed to us here was addressed to the Court for the purpose of showing that a person who had bought a certain number of tons of sugar, part of a larger stock, had no insurable interest in the quantity bought, because bags had been appropriated to the contract and consequently the property in them had not passed. But as Lord Blackburn there pointed out, although the purchaser did not acquire the property in any particular number of tons of sugar he did acquire an undivided interest in the larger bulk and that undivided interest the House of Lords held to be insurable. The acquisition of an undivided interest in a larger bulk clearly will not suffice to pass the property when the appropriation to the contract has to be made by the vendor himself. As Baron Bayley said in *Gillett* v. *Hill*: 'Where there is a bargain for a certain quantity' of goods 'ex a greater quantity, and there is a power of selection in the vendor to deliver which he thinks fit, then the right to them does not pass to the vendee until the vendor has made his selection, and trover is not maintainable before that is done.' Nor probably will the acquisition of such an undivided interest pass the property, so as to entitle the purchaser to sue for a conversion, in a case where the power of appropriation is, as here, in a third party. But in that latter case, whether the property passes or not, the transfer of the undivided interest carries with it the risk of loss from something happening to the goods, such as a deterioration in their quality, at all events after the vendor has given the purchaser a delivery order upon the party in possession of them, and that party has assented to it. The vendor of a specified quantity out of a bulk in the possession of a third party discharges his obligation to the purchaser as soon as the third party undertakes to the purchaser to deliver him that quantity out of the bulk."

Again in *Healy* v. *Howlett & Sons* [1917 1 K.B. 337] where the question arose as to the passing of property in a consignment of 190 boxes of mackerel which had been put on rail to answer the contracts of the defendant and two other consignees, the contention that the property had passed was rejected. At page 342 the argument advanced was: "As to the property passing to the defendants, when the mackerel were delivered to the railway company at Valentia the defendants and the two other consignees had from that moment an undivided interest in the goods, and after they arrived at Holyhead each consignee would have been entitled to claim the specific boxes which had been allocated to them if they had chosen to go to Holyhead. That consideration shows that the property had passed to the defendants." That was rejected by Mr. Justice Ridley who said (at page 344): "There are insuperable difficulties in holding that the property has passed in the present case. It is impossible to say which consignee is to bear the loss caused by the deterioration of any particular boxes of the mackerel. The essence of the authorities which decide that appropriation of goods to the contract by delivery to the carrier at the beginning of the transit may be sufficient to pass the property is that it should be known to whom the goods are appropriated, and not that the question as to who is to bear any loss that may happen should be open to any discussion or be determined by the accident." And Mr. Justice Avory in his judgment says: "I agree that *Stock* v. *Inglis* does not govern the present case, though at first sight it might appear to involve the same question. That it involved a very different question is I think clear from the language of Lord Blackburn," and then he quotes the passage "That shows," he says, "that for the purpose of that case all that was necessary to hold was that the plaintiff had as against the insurance company an undivided interest in the parcel of goods which was on board the ship, a totally different matter from deciding that he has the property in a particular twenty boxes out of a consignment of 190, when, as in the present case, nobody can possibly tell which twenty out of the 190 belonged to the defendants and which boxes belonged to the other purchasers."

I think, with Mr. Justice Ridley that there are insuperable difficulties in the way of Mr. Wright's argument, but even if I am wrong about that, I think that the same objection applies here as in the case of Mr. Strong. Even if Mr. Wright's argument is correct as a matter of law, its underlying basis must be that there is an identifiable whole which has been appropriated in some way to answer for the quantities which it is said exhaust the entire parcel. That simply does not appear to me to be the case here. I cannot construe the words "lying in bond" as providing an identifying label for the mass from which the goods were to be selected. In my view, the Company remained free to fulfil the contracts to its various purchasers from any source, as, for instance, by importing further wine of the same description. That being so, the mere fact that the Company sold quantities of wine which in fact exhausted all the stocks which it held cannot, in my judgment, have had the effect of passing a proprietary interest in those stocks to the various purchasers so that they can now claim the goods collectively and ignore the Bank's charge.

In the case of the third category of purchaser, represented by Mr. Bailey and by Vinum Ltd. and their respective pledgees, the case is put rather differently. It is not contended that any proprietary interest passed at law, but what is said is that an interest by estoppel was vested in the purchasers. The principles are enunciated in a number of cases such as *Stonard* v. *Dunkin* [2 Camp. 344], *Woodley* v. *Coventry*,

[2 Hurl. & Colt. 164] and *Knights* v. *Wiffen* [L.R. 5 Q.B. 660], and are usefully summarised in paragraph 346 of Benjamin on Sale of Goods: "Where the bulk from which the goods are to be taken is in possession of a third person such as a warehouseman, the acceptance by the warehouseman of a delivery order given by the seller to the buyer, and even the transfer of the goods to be sold into the name of the buyer in his books, will not pass the property in the goods to the buyer while they are still unascertained. But if the seller gives a delivery order to the buyer, or the buyer gives a delivery order to the sub-purchaser, then a confirmation of the delivery order by the seller or the warehouseman may estop them from denying that the property has passed. In order, however, for such an estoppel to arise, there must be a representation by words or conduct that the buyer or sub-purchaser is entitled to the goods, the mere receipt of a delivery order without any acknowledgment will not suffice. It must also be shown that the position of the buyer or sub-purchaser has therefore been prejudiced. Estoppel does not in itself pass the property of the goods, but the buyer or sub-purchaser is entitled to maintain an action for conversion if the goods are not delivered to him, and the seller is precluded from setting up an unpaid seller's lien."

In the case of Mr. Bailey, the correspondence exhibited shows how, in very many cases, the Company, at the instance of the pledgee from the purchaser, invited the warehouseman to issue warehouse receipts acknowledging that he held wine to the account of the pledgee. The case of Compass is even clearer, for here there was a master agreement to which the Company was a party and under which it warranted the validity of the warehouse receipts and that the wine held by it was a custodian for the pledgor.

There is no doubt that the pledgees were intended to and did alter their position on the faith of these representations by advancing money to Mr. Bailey and Vinum Ltd. respectively.

In these circumstances Mr. Wright on behalf of Mr. Bailey and Mr. Stamler on behalf of Vinum Ltd. and its pledgees submit that both the Company and the warehouseman are estopped and that there was created in the purchasers and their pledgees proprietary interests by estoppel created before the Bank's charge crystallised and so binding upon it.

None of the warehousemen is a party to these proceedings so that nothing that I say would be binding upon them in any event but in fact I cannot see how an estoppel affecting the warehousemen could affect the Bank except in so far as such an estoppel created a proprietary interest in the goods in the warehouse subject to which the Bank's charge takes effect. But the authorities to which I have referred above make one thing quite clear and that is that no property *actually* passes, although the estoppel operates to enable the plaintiff to prosecute an action in trover in which he can obtain damages from the warehouseman.

The real questions, as it seems to me, are:

(i) are the circumstances such as to create an estoppel against the Company, and
(ii) if so, does that estoppel affect the Bank?

As to the first point Mr. Stamler submits that the estoppel can operate not only against the warehouseman but also against the seller, at any rate if, as here, the seller was a party to the representation. That I think must be right. There is no magic in the fact that the representation is made by a bailee and indeed *Knights* v. *Wiffen* was a case where the seller of unascertained goods was estopped by his assent to the buyer's delivery order from denying that he had appropriated goods to the contract.

It is the second question which causes the difficulty.

What Mr. Stamler seeks to do is to establish by estoppel a proprietary interest by way of charge on the Company's goods which takes effect in priority to the Bank's charge. The way in which he puts it is this: given a representation by the Company that goods have been appropriated to the contract and given that that was acted upon by the lender in lending his money (and indeed by the borrower in borrowing it) the only ingredient lacking from a complete title in both borrower and lender is the specific property. If, at the stage immediately before the representation is acted upon, there is no prior charge, so that the only person in whom the right rests to complete or not to complete the contract is the V.endor, he can complete in two ways, that is to say either by making an actual appropriation or by putting himself in a position in which he is to be treated as having made an appropriation. When the representation is acted upon he is put in this position and from that moment the titles of lender and borrower are complete.

Mr. Bingham on behalf of the Bank, has submitted that even if this were right the Bank's Charge takes priority because a floating charge is still a charge from the inception and can be ousted only by a completed disposition of the assets charged before crystallisation. But I doubt whether the problem in this case is easily answered by reference to the juristic nature of a floating charge, interesting though that question be. If the true analysis be—and this is certainly the view which emerges from the earlier cases—that there is, from the inception, a charge but subject to a licence to the Company to dispose of the assets charged in the ordinary course of business, the question still remains: what is embraced by the licence and does it cover a disposition by estoppel?

The real difficulty in Mr. Stamler's way seems to me to be the nature of the estoppel upon which he is compelled to rely. It is certainly clear from the decision of the Court of Appeal in *Eastern Distributors Ltd.* v. *Goldring* [1957 2 Q.B. 600] that in the case of a sale of specific goods by an agent within the scope of his apparent authority the estoppel (if it be an estoppel) of the principal affects third parties claiming to derive title from the principle under a subsequent transaction. But it must be borne in mind that in that case the Court doubted whether this was truly a case of estoppel at all and based the decision rather on a common law rule, evolved as a matter of commercial convenience, under which the *actual* title passed to the buyer just as in the case of a transferee of a negotiable instrument or a buyer in market overt. But even allowing (i) that the principle of the *Eastern Distributors* case is applicable in a wider field than that of sale of specific goods under apparent authority and (ii) that the Bank's charge takes effect only from the date of crystallisation, the question remains: what is it that the Company is estopped from denying and how is the Bank affected by it?

A person who lends money to a Company on the security of a debenture containing a floating charge does not, when his charge crystallises, become universal successor of the borrower like a trustee in bankruptcy or a personal representative so as to subject himself to all claims which may lie against the borrower, although, of course, as an equitable assignee of the assets he is in no better position than a trustee or liquidator would be as regards the assets assigned. He is a chargee of the borrower's assets who has, under powers contained in his contract, appointed someone to manage the Company, and he takes the assets subject to any proprietary rights or incumbrances (including rights of set-off) in third parties which may legitimately have been created by the borrower in those assets within the terms of the debenture. But to say that he is "in no better position than" a liquidator or trustee in bankruptcy is to express it too widely if those words are taken out of the context in which they were used in the case of *Barker* v. *Eynon*. The lender does not become subject to all the personal claims to which the borrower may have subjected himself in the course of running his business.

The difficulty that I feel with regard to both Mr. Stamler's and Mr. Wright's submissions is in seeing how the fact that the Company may have estopped itself by its representations from denying that it has appropriated goods to the contract, when it has not done so in fact, can confer any proprietary interest upon the representee in any goods of the Company becoming subject to the Bank's charge, for as it appears to me, the only right which can be asserted as arising from the estoppel is one to damages.

The essence of an estoppel is that the truth is not allowed to be told, and when one talks of a "title by estoppel" one is not, in truth, talking about a title at all. It is indeed inherent in the concept that there is not title but the representor is not allowed to say so. As Lord

Justice Farwell puts it in *Bank of England* v. *Cutler* [1908 2 K.B. 208] at page 234: "It is true that a title by estoppel is only good against the person estopped and imports from its very existence the idea of no real title at all, yet as against the person estopped it has all the elements of a real title."

In none of the cases to which I have been referred in which a vendor or warehouseman was held to be estopped from denying that an appropriation had taken place was any actual interest conferred on the representee and it is difficult to see how it could be. What happened was that the representor was not allowed to deny that he had goods belonging to the representee and he was accordingly made to pay damages in an action of trover.

Now it is far from clear that an innocent purchaser even of specific goods can be affected by an estoppel affecting his seller in relation to those goods. The point was touched on in the *Eastern Distributors* case and the Court of Appeal did little to encourage the idea. At page 606, Mr. Justice Devlin (as he then was) who delivered the judgment of the Court said this: "An estoppel affects others besides the representor, The way it has always been put is that the estoppel binds the representor and his privies. But it is not easy to determine exactly who for this purpose is a privy. There can be no doubt that although the representation was actually made by Coker, Murphy on the facts of this case was privy to the making and is bound by it: see *Downs* v. *Cooper* [1841 2 Q.B. 256]. It would also appear that anyone whose title is obtained from the representor as a volunteer is a privy for this purpose. But it is very doubtful whether a purchaser for value without notice is bound by the estoppel. The point is fully discussed in Ewart on Estoppel by Misrepresentation (1900) pp. 199–203, and the author concludes that a purchaser for value without notice is not bound. This part of the doctrine of estoppel has been worked out by courts of equity and chiefly in relation to the sale of land. There is no trace of its application to contracts for the sale of goods."

In the case of unascertained goods the concept of a subsequent purchaser or incumbrancer as a privy is even more difficult to apply. The seller is, by assumption, estopped from denying that he has sold and appropriated to the contract a given quantity of goods of a particular description but it is very difficult to see why this estoppel should affect a third party merely because he has purchased from the seller or obtained a charge on goods of that same description. Even if it did, the fact that the purchaser or chargee is precluded from denying that the seller has sold a specified quantity of goods to the representee would still not preclude him from claiming as his the goods which were actually sold or charged to him and to which he has the real title.

If I may adopt the words of Mr. Justice Romer in *Robson* v. *Smith*

[1895 2 Ch. 124]: "So long as the debentures remain a mere floating security, or, in other words, the licence to the Company to carry on its business has not been terminated, the property of the Company may be dealt with in the ordinary course of business as if the debentures had not been given, and any such dealing with a particular property will be binding on the debenture-holders, provided that the dealing be completed before the debentures cease to be a mere floating charge."

But, of course, when one is dealing with a situation in which an estoppel is said to arise from a representation or appropriation, then *ex hypothesi* the dealing has not been completed and no outside interest has in fact been created in the vendor's property by the uncompleted dealing. With one exception no authority to which I have been referred or which I have been able to find suggests that the estoppel in such circumstances confers upon the representee some interest in the vendor's property *in specie* which he can assert either against the vendor himself or against a third party to whom may have been transferred the title to or an interest in the property of the vendor at the time when the uncompleted dealing took place.

The exception is an *obiter dictum* of Lord Justice Cotton in *Simm* v. *Anglo-American Telegraph Company*, [5 Q.B.D. 188] a case which was concerned with an estoppel arising from a forged transfer of shares which had been registered by the Company. The shares had been pledged to a Bank against which the Company was clearly estopped by the issue of the share certificate, but the question was whether that estoppel could, after the Bank had been paid off, enure for the benefit of the shareholder who had got his registration on the faith of the forged transfer. In other words, did the estoppel against the Bank create a title? The Court of Appeal answered this question in the negative but there is a passage in the judgment of Lord Justice Cotton which seems to suggest that in circumstances such as the present an actual title might be conferred. He said this at page 215: "As I understand the question, a good title by estoppel may exist in some cases: for instance, by indenture a lease for years may be granted of land in which at the time the lessor has no interest, but if he afterwards acquires a sufficient interest to support the lease, by estoppel it becomes valid for the term created and the lessee has a good title to the subject-matter of demise. There may be also a good title by estoppel to things which do not require any instrument to transfer them, as for instance, goods: if an action is brought upon the ground that the property in goods has passed to the vendor of the plaintiff, and if that question depends upon whether a particular parcel of goods has been set apart and appropriated to the contract between the vendor of the plaintiff and the defendant, an admission by the defendant, the owner of the goods, that there had been a setting apart of the goods, would be effectual as against him to pass the property in the goods to the plaintiff's vendor: as against the plaintiff who has paid for the goods, the defendant is estopped from denying that the goods have been set apart, and the plaintiff is entitled to rely upon the admission of the defendant, which if true would have given the plaintiff a good title to the goods. A case of that description is *Knights* v. *Wiffen*."

Now if by this Lord Justice Cotton was intending to suggest that a representation of appropriation carried an *actual* title to the goods, this certainly does not seem to have been the view of Lord Esher, to whose judgment I will refer in a moment. But I do not think that he was. At an earlier point in his judgment he had referred to what he meant when he spoke of "title by estoppel." At page 213 he said: "I will first consider what is the meaning of the words 'title by estoppel' or if that phrase be objected to, 'right by estoppel.' As I understand, it means that where one person makes to another a statement which is afterwards acted upon, in any action afterwards brought upon the faith of that statement by the person to whom it was made, the person making it is not allowed to deny that the facts were what he represented them to be, although in truth they were different." In the passage to which I have previously referred he clearly had in mind the *Knights* v. *Wiffen* situation and indeed expressly refers to that case. But unless he had misread *Knights* v. *Wiffen*, I do not think that he could have regarded the estoppel in that case as conferring an *actual* title on the plaintiff's vendor. One has only to look at the report of *Knights* v. *Wiffen* to see that it clearly did not decide that. Knights, the Plaintiff, was a sub-purchaser from Maris who had purchased from the Defendant; and the representation was made to Knights, not to Maris.

At page 664 of the report Mr. Justice Blackburn says this: "The station-master went to Wiffen and showed him the delivery order and letter, and Wiffen said, 'All right, when you receive the forwarding note, I will place the barley on the line.' What does that mean? It amounts to this, that Maris having given the order to enable Knights to obtain the barley, Wiffen recognised Knights as the person entitled to the possession of it, Knights had handed the delivery-order to the station-master, and Wiffen, when the document was shown to him, said, in effect, 'It is quite right; I have sixty quarters of barley to Maris' order, I will hold it for you; and when the forwarding-note comes I will put it on the railway for you.' Upon that statement Knights rested assured, and Wiffen, by accepting the transfer which had been informally addressed to the station-master, bound himself to Knights. The latter accordingly, when he did not get the goods, brought an action of trover against Wiffen."

"No doubt," he goes on at page 665, "the law is that until an appropriation from a bulk is made, so that the vendor has said what portion belongs to him and what portion belongs to the buyer, the goods remain in solido, and no property passes. But can Wiffen here be permitted to say, 'I never set aside any quarters'? As to that *Woodley* v. *Coventry* is very much in point."

Mr. Justice Mellor quoted from Blackburn of Sale, and he said this: "This is a rule, which, within the limits applied by law, is of great equity; for when parties have agreed to act upon an assumed state of facts, their rights between themselves are justly made to depend on the conventional state of facts and not on the truth. The reason of the rule ceases at once when a stranger to the arrangement seeks to avail himself of the statements which were not made as a basis for him to act upon. They are for a stranger evidence against the party making the statement, but no more than evidence which may be rebutted; between the parties they form an estoppel in law." Mr. Justice Lush considered the case indistinguishable from *Woodley* v. *Coventry* [2 Hurl. & Colt. 164].

Now in that case, the one thing that is abundantly clear is that the Court was not saying that the estoppel created by the representation to the Plaintiff sub-purchaser conferred a title on the plaintiff's vendor, in that case a Mr. Clarke, and, indeed two members of the Court went out of their way to say so.

At page 171 Baron Martin says: "I think, upon the authority of *Hawes* v. *Watson*, that the question is not whether Clarke was the owner of the flour, but whether, as between the plaintiffs and the defendants, the latter must not be taken to have assented that there were 348 barrels of flour at their warehouse deliverable to the plaintiffs' order; and if so, the property attached in the sense that the defendants are precluded in a Court of Law from denying that they held that number of barrels on the plaintiffs' account. In strictness, the question whether the defendants assented is one of fact for the jury." And Chief Baron Pollock at page 174 said: "The real question was whether the defendants had so conducted themselves that the plaintiffs had a right to say, 'We call upon you to deliver to us the flour which you say you held on our behalf.' The question whether the property passed, as between vendor and vendee, never arose: the only question was whether the defendants had acknowledged that they held the flour on behalf of the plaintiffs, for, if so, according to law and justice, they were bound to deliver it or pay the damages." *Woodley* v. *Coventry* had been cited in the argument in *Simm's* case and possibly Lord Justice Cotton may have had in mind the following passage from the judgment of Baron Bramwell in the former case where he said this: "Mr. Williams says that the effect of the transaction is not that which I have suggested, but merely to give Clarke a right to demand the delivery of a certain number of barrels of flour, and which right he transferred to the plaintiffs. But that is not so. When the delivery order was presented to the defendants, they might have said, "We will not accept this order, for there are not 348 barrels of flour in our warehouse of which Clarke has a right to dispose. There is a much larger quantity in the warehouse out of which Clarke has a right to 348 when selected and appropriated to him, but, until that is done, he has no right to any, for they are not his.' But instead of saying that, the defendants in effect say, 'We recognise a right in Clarke to dispose of 348 barrels,' which could only be upon the supposition that the property in 348 barrels had passed to him."

But again, it is clear I think that Baron Bramwell did not consider that this could have conferred any actual title to the goods because he goes on to consider what would have been the position if the goods had been destroyed, and at page 173 he says this: "Mr. Williams has also suggested that we ought not only to look at the result of the evidence, but also consider what would have been the position of the parties if the flour had been burnt. Perhaps, in that case, the defendants would have had to bear the loss, because there was no appropriation of the flour; but it is unnecessary to consider whether or not they would have been entitled to be paid for it." And a little further down in discussing who was at fault, he says: "While, however, in one sense they were not in fault, in another sense they were, for by recognising the order they placed themselves in the difficulty which has been suggested of having no remedy against the plaintiffs if the goods were burnt, and nevertheless being liable in this action." So he was clearly considering the case on the footing that the property had not passed.

Certainly Lord Justice Brett (as he then was) in the *Simm's* case did not consider that there was any question of any property passing. At page 206 he says this: "The doctrine of estoppel was recognised in Courts of Common Law just as much as it was in the Courts of Equity, and it seems to me that an estoppel gives no title to that which is the subject-matter of estoppel. The estoppel assumes that the reality is contrary to that which the person is estopped from denying, and the estoppel has no effect at all upon the reality of the circumstances. I speak not of that estoppel, which is said to arise upon a deed of conveyance or other deed of a similar nature. I incline to think that when the word 'estoppel' is used with reference to deeds of that kind, it is merely a phrase indicating that they must be truly interpreted. I am speaking now of the estoppels which arise upon transactions in business or in daily life, and, as it seems to me, these estoppels have no effect on the reality of the transaction. It may be that under some circumstances an estoppel will prevent a person from dealing in a particular manner with goods; for instance, if a person is estopped from denying that he has made a contract to deliver goods, and if the goods are still in his possession, in a suit to enforce performance of the alleged contract he may be obliged to hand over the goods, although, in fact, there was no contract, and he may be liable to act as if there had been a contract, and to fulfil his supposed obligation. But suppose that although a person is estopped from denying that he has made a contract to deliver goods, he has parted with the goods and has sold them to somebody else; it seems to me that although he may be estopped as against the person claiming delivery under the supposed contract, he cannot be compelled to deliver the goods, which, there being no contract, have legally passed to somebody else: owing to the estoppel he cannot deny that a contract was entered into, but he cannot fulfil it by delivering another person's goods; and therefore the only remedy against him is that he shall pay damages for not delivering the goods. In a similar manner a person may be estopped from denying that certain goods belong to another; he may be compelled by a suit in the nature of an action of trover to deliver them up, if he has them in his possession and under his control; but if the goods, in respect of which he has estopped himself, really belong to somebody else, it seems impossible to suppose that by any process of law he can be compelled to deliver over another's goods to the person in whose favour the estoppel exists against him: that person is entitled to maintain a suit in the nature of an action of trover against him; but that person cannot recover the goods, because no property has really passed to him, he can recover only damages. In my view estoppel has no effect upon the real nature of the transaction: it only creates a cause of action between the person in whose favour the estoppel exists and the person who is estopped."

This, as it seems to me, accords with the views expressed in *Knights* v. *Wiffen* and *Woodley* v. *Coventry*, and if so and so far as there is a conflict between the views of Lord Esher and Lord Justice Cotton, those of the former appear to me to accord more with what I understand to be the true nature and effect of an estoppel by representation.

I can find here no estoppel which, in my judgment, can affect the Bank or preclude it from asserting its real title to the assets of the Company at the relevant date. Mr. Stamler did at one stage suggest that Compass might be in a position different from and stronger than that of Vinum Ltd. in as much as it had a lien upon the goods, perfected by the attornment of the warehouseman.

No doubt a general lien existing before crystallisation of a floating charge will prevail over the claim of the debenture-holder—this seems clear from *Brunton* v. *Electrical Engineering Corporation* [1892 1 Ch. 434], which was approved in *George Barker Ltd.* v. *Eynon* [1974 1 All E.R. 900].

But here Compass's lien, if that is the right word, arose from the attempted pledge of the goods.

Quite apart from the question whether the creation of a pledge on the Company's goods amounts to the creation of a charge ranking *pari passu* with or in priority to the floating charge—a dealing specifically prohibited by the debenture—a lien must depend upon the person having the lien being in possession, which Compass never had in reality, So that the argument here is again based on an estoppel of the warehouseman and the same questions arise as have already been mentioned above with regard to the position of a person not a party to the estoppel.

Accordingly, I have felt compelled, perhaps rather reluctantly, to the conclusion that I must direct: (1) that all three categories of goods described in the Schedule to the Summons should be dealt with by the Receiver as being the property of the Company on the relevant date and so subject to the floating charge and (2) that no such goods are subject to any lien or other interest having priority to the floating charge in favour of the Respondent purchasers or their respective assigns or mortgagees.

MR. JUSTICE OLIVER: Now, I have not there dealt with the position of the fourth category.

MR. MORRIS SMITH: My Lord, I will not myself be seeking leave to add Mr. Polk(?) as a Respondent in place of Mrs. Pilkington or at all. In so far as the Receiver is concerned I understand the Receiver will be satisfied for the Bank to say to him: "We do not pay the charge on those goods ————

MR. JUSTICE OLIVER: Of course the questions which will arise in any individual case would be ones where the goods have in fact been appropriated to the contract, but that must necessarily of course I suppose vary with the individual circumstances.

MR. MORRIS SMITH: Yes, unless ————

MR. JUSTICE OLIVER: Indeed, if the Summons proceeds upon the footing in all the other categories that there has been no appropriation, and that is the supposition upon which the whole Summons is based.

MR. MORRIS SMITH: That is so, my Lord. As I say, I do not think myself, that I would have asked that there be an additional Respondent, Mr. Polk (?) added. Your Lordship in your Lordship's judgment dealt with category (b) for very obvious reasons.

MR. JUSTICE OLIVER: No, there remains, Mr. Morris Smith, the question of representation I think.

MR. MORRIS SMITH: That is so, my Lord. Of course, your Lordship has in effect found against all the representative classes or against all the parties who have sought to be made representatives, and I would ask for order to be made in respect of paragraph 2, sub-paragraphs (1), (2) and (3) of the Summons.

MR. JUSTICE OLIVER: I tell you the difficulty I feel about that. You see, it has been impossible for obvious reasons to introduce evidence showing what happened in the case of each individual purchaser. If I am going to make a Representation Order which is going to bind everybody, I would be most reluctant to make anything which is going to bar people from raising individual circumstances in their own given particular cases which may not perhaps apply in the case we are dealing with. Is it not enough for the Receiver to treat the judgment as a guidance for other cases?

MR. MORRIS SMITH: I think it would be, my Lord. As to your Lordship's point, which I fully accept, that one does not want to bind other purchasers who have special circumstances different as between themselves, I would submit that of course a Representative Order made under Order 15:12 in the Annual Practice which is page 202—I need not perhaps ask your Lordship to read the provisions there upon which a Representation Order was made—but taking your Lordship's specific point, if your Lordship turns to sub-paragraph (5) of Rule 12: "Notwithstanding that a judgment or order to which any such application relates is binding on the person against whom the application is made, that person may dispute liability to have the judgment or order enforced against him of the ground that by reason of facts and matters particular to his case he is entitled to be exempted from such liability."

MR. JUSTICE OLIVER: Oh yes, I had not seen that. That really overcomes the objection that I was raising, I would think, does it not? Mr. Wright, you appear for ————

MR. WRIGHT: Yes, my Lord, I would have thought because of that Order there would be no objection to a Representation Order. It probably makes the judgment slightly more authoritative.

MR. JUSTICE OLIVER: It would be helpful from the Receiver's point of view obviously if he has got a Representation Order which binds everybody. There is no difficulty, I think, to my making a Representation Order simply because they happen to come under a specific statutory provision of the Companies Act, is there? Order 15, Rule 12 is perfectly germane to this application, I think.

MR. MORRIS SMITH: I think so, my Lord. There is nothing so far as I am aware enacted in regard to proceedings under the Companies Act in the Winding-up Rules or otherwise as regards representation.

MR. WRIGHT: The Rules of the Supreme Court apply unless otherwise provided.

MR. JUSTICE OLIVER: That is right, Very well then I will make ———

MR. MORRIS SMITH: My Lord, first of all, perhaps a minor point, if your Lordship is minded to make an order under paragraph 2, when one comes to 3: "all purchasers of wine," that is a category C case, my Lord. Of course Mr. Bailey was originally the only member, and if the order is sought that he should represent all those, I think one perhaps should insert: "all purchasers not being Respondents hereto."

MR. JUSTICE OLIVER: I think that is right because Vinum and its category are bound in their own right.

MR. MORRIS SMITH: The extent of the Representation Order, if I might perhaps trespass on your Lordship's lenience on this, of course your Lordship has dealt fully perhaps in the forefront of your Lordship's judgment with the argument that the trust(?) is based on the letter, Certificate of Title. That is not in fact a document specifically referred to in any of the descriptions of the classes. It is conceivable from the Receiver's point of view that another purchaser might come along and say: "I am not within any of your three classes. I was sent a letter saying that I was a purchaser of these wines and I was the beneficial owner. And I know if you obtain judgment saying that that would be an argument which would fail, that I am not bound by it."

MR. JUSTICE OLIVER: I see, you really want to add into the category something after the words: "no acknowledgment by the Company other than the common form letter," or something of that sort.

MR. MORRIS SMITH: I think my client would be covered if one added to category (c) as it stands—this is Mr. Bailey—and it reads at the moment: "in respect of which before the relevant date there was no act of appropriation but an acknowledgment as aforesaid was given to the purchaser or his assign or mortgagee" add then the words: "or before the relevant date a letter of the Company was written acknowledging the title or beneficial ownership of the purchaser to or in wine answering that description." So one then has Mr. Bailey bound by your Lordship's judgment on behalf of others of his category, say there were instances where there was no act of appropriation, there was either an acknowledgment, which your Lordship of course dealt with, or alternatively there was this letter.

MR. JUSTICE OLIVER: Yes, I see, one does not need to have a similar formula in the other two cases.

MR. MORRIS SMITH: No, but the other two are very special—of course your Lordship's judgment applies to them individually so far as they received letters of entitlement, but they are special cases in the sense that the parts of your Lordship's judgment which are special to them is this question of whether a purchaser of the whole of the stock could be summoned, and from the Receiver's point of view, if one got it under any category, there is a class bound by the decision as to the effect of the letter of entitlement.

MR. JUSTICE OLIVER: Yes, I see, if you put it in the alternative, that: "an acknowledgment as aforesaid was given to the purchaser or his assign or before" . . . yes, that is it, that would cover all cases, I think.

MR. MORRIS SMITH: If your Lordship would concur that that would be proper, then your Lordship would perhaps give me leave to amend the Summons in relation to category (c).

MR. JUSTICE OLIVER: Yes, I would. Is there any objection to this?

MR. (?) [*Name not identified on transcript*]: No, my Lord, I was just thinking why it was not thought necessary in categories (a) and (b)?

MR. JUSTICE OLIVER: Because I think Mr. Morris Smith would say that if you put it in (c) then (a) and (b) are going to be within (c) for this purpose, because they will be equal, you see.

MR. (?): My Lord, this does not affect me, My Lord, it does occur to me just listening to my learned friend that it could have made a difference of your Lordship's judgment what the letter had said, and if somebody turned up with a different letter ———

MR. JUSTICE OLIVER: Yes, that is quite right, but I think we have to define the letter by reference to the ones which are in evidence which are in fact in the same form.

MR. (?): My Lord, that is all I was mentioning, and I do not think my learned friend did that; I may have misheard him.

MR. MORRIS SMITH: No, I do not in fact ———

MR. JUSTICE OLIVER: Mr. Morris Smith, it is terribly difficult for you to, as it were, draft on your feet. Would it not be easier for you to formulate the amendment and lodge a Minute with the Registrar?

MR. MORRIS SMITH: If your Lordship pleases.

MR. JUSTICE OLIVER: Because it may be a quite complicated order to draw if we have got to incorporate reference to an amended Summons.

MR. MORRIS SMITH: Yes, I would be very happy if the matter could be left to be dealt with in that way, my Lord.

MR. JUSTICE OLIVER: I think it would probably be easier if it were left to be dealt with in that way. I do not know if anyone has got any better ideas.

MR. MORRIS SMITH: Subject to that amendment the representation orders would be made slightly amended as regards subparagraph (3) of paragraph 2 of the Summons, that there were three representations.

MR. JUSTICE OLIVER: That is right.

MR. MORRIS SMITH: Then there, of course, remains the question of costs. As far as the Receiver is concerned I would submit that their costs in the receivership would be ordered to be paid as such. If necessary I will endeavour to debate this, but I think it is the position that the Receiver's costs on an indemnity basis should be costs in the Receivership. As for the costs of the other Respondents, I think perhaps it is a matter for them.

MR. JUSTICE OLIVER: It will be between Mr. Bingham, Mr. Reynold and Mr. Wright.

MR. (?): My Lord, I had understood this anyhow to be the common case, in my submission, that as one was going to deal with these matters at the instance of a Receiver, it ought to be all of them should be paid out of the Fund, or out of the Receivership as costs of the Receivership on a common fund basis.

MR. JUSTICE OLIVER: Mr. Bingham, what is your client's attitude as to costs?

MR. BINGHAM: My Lord, I would ask for my costs to come out of the Fund.

MR. JUSTICE OLIVER: Certainly your costs would (*Laughter*).

MR. BINGHAM: My Lord, so far as the other two parties are concerned, my instructions are neither to support nor to oppose the application that is made. We regard it as a question very much for your Lordship.

MR. JUSTICE OLIVER: Yes, I would have thought that in a case of this sort surely a Receiver had to come to the Court in the circumstances. It was clearly right that somebody should be joined to argue these things, because I could not have decided the case without argument, and I would have thought it would be right that they should have their costs. The only thing that is bothering me is the question of Mr. Reynold's costs, because we have already had a person joined to represent the pledged class as it were, and Mr. Reynold's clients joined at their own request. What do you say, Mr. Reynold?

MR. REYNOLD (for Mr. Stamler): My Lord, I would say that it was entirely right and proper that they should have been joined albeit at their invitation. In fact, in my submission, it would have been probably prudent to have joined by them in the first place. They are far and away the largest single investor. Your Lordship has the figures as to the extent of their investment. Their interest in the outcome of these proceedings was considerable, and indeed it was appropriate that they should have separate representation.

MR. JUSTICE OLIVER: In the sense, that there was in their case a different set of documents.

MR. REYNOLD: Relating to the pledge and documents relating to Compass.

MR. JUSTICE OLIVER: It was not until today that anybody knew what answer the Court would give.

MR. REYNOLD: Indeed, my Lord, it was wholly right that they should become a party to these proceedings whether at their invitation or at the insistence of the Receiver, and it would defeat the justice of the case if your Lordship did not differentiate between their position and my learned friend, Mr. Wright.

MR. JUSTICE OLIVER: I think that must be right, Mr. Reynold, and Mr. Bingham's attitude happily agrees. What I would propose is I think the Receiver probably ought to have his costs on a trustee basis, should he not, Mr. Morris Smith?

MR. MORRIS SMITH: I think that is so, my Lord, yes.

MR. JUSTICE OLIVER: So I will direct the Receiver's costs and expenses to be taxed and the costs of the other parties to be taxed on a common fund basis and paid out of the Fund. When I say "Fund," I think it should be the funds that the Receiver has.

MR. MORRIS SMITH: Yes, they of course would be subject to the charge ————

MR. JUSTICE OLIVER: Yes, subject to the charge. That now covers everything on the Fund. We do not need to do anything about the fourth Respondent or the fifth Respondent?

MR. MORRIS SMITH: I did understand that the order was all the Respondents including the fourth.

MR. JUSTICE OLIVER: I think that is right. It turned out that the fourth Respondent's case did not arise. Nobody knew that at the time. I think it should be all the Respondents. In fact I do not suppose that there are any additional costs, because you represent the lot. Very well.

INDEX